African Christianity

Zapf Chancery Tertiary Level Publications

A Guide to Academic Writing by C. B. Peter (1994)
Africa in the 21st Century by Eric M. Aseka (1996)
Women in Development by Egara Kabaji (1997)
Introducing Social Science: A Guidebook by J. H. van Doorne (2000)
Elementary Statistics by J. H. van Doorne (2001)
Iteso Survival Rites on the Birth of Twins by Festus B. Omusolo (2001)
The Church in the New Millennium: Three Studies in the Acts of the Apostles by John Stott (2002)
Introduction to Philosophy in an African Perspective by Cletus N.Chukwu (2002)
Participatory Monitoring and Evaluation by Francis W. Mulwa and Simon N. Nguluu (2003)
Applied Ethics and HIV/AIDS in Africa by Cletus N. Chukwu (2003)
For God and Humanity: 100 Years of St. Paul's United Theological College Edited by Emily Onyango (2003)
Establishing and Managing School Libraries and Resource Centres by Margaret Makenzi and Raymond Ongus (2003)
Introduction to the Study of Religion by Nehemiah Nyaundi (2003)
A Guest in God's World: Memories of Madagascar by Patricia McGregor (2004)
Introduction to Critical Thinking by J. Kahiga Kiruki (2004)
Theological Education in Contemporary Africa edited by GrantLeMarquand and Joseph D. Galgalo (2004)
Looking Religion in the Eye edited by Kennedy Onkware (2004)
Computer Programming: Theory and Practice by Gerald Injendi (2005)
Demystifying Participatory Development by Francis W. Mulwa (2005)
Music Education in Kenya: A Historical Perspective by Hellen A. Odwar (2005)
Into the Sunshine: Integrating HIV/AIDS into Ethics Curriculum Edited by Charles Klagba and C. B. Peter (2005)
Integrating HIV/AIDS into Ethics Curriculum: Suggested Modules Edited by Charles Klagba (2005)
Dying Voice (An Anthropological Novel) by Andrew K. Tanui (2006)
Participatory Learning and Action (PLA): A Guide to Best Practice by Enoch Harun Opuka (2006)
Science and Human Values: Essays in Science, Religion, and Modern Ethical Issues edited by Nehemiah Nyaundi and Kennedy Onkware (2006)
Understanding Adolescent Behaviour by Daniel Kasomo (2006)
Students' Handbook for Guidance and Counselling by Daniel Kasomo (2007)
BusinessOrganization and Management: Questions and Answers by Musa O. Nyakora (2007)
Auditing Priniples: A Stuents' Handbook by Musa O. Nyakora (2007)
The Concept of Botho and HIV/AIDS in Botswana edite by Joseph B. R. Gaie and Sana K. MMolai (2007)
Captive of Fate: A Novel by Ketty Arucy (2007)
A Guide to Ethics by Joseph Njino (2008)
An Introduction to Philosophy of Religion by John M. M. Kasyoka (2008)
Pastoral Theology: Rediscovering African Models and Methods by John Ndung'u Ikenye (2009)

(Continued after Index)

African Christianity
The Stranger Within

Joseph D. Galgalo PhD (Cantab)

***Zapf Chancery*
Limuru, Kenya**

First Published 2012
©Joseph Galgalo
All rights reserved.

Cover Concept and Design
Joseph Galgalo and C. B. Peter

Associate Designer and Typesetter
Nancy Njeri

Copyediting
C. B. Peter

Editor and Publishing Consultant
C. B. Peter

Printed by
Kijabe Printing Press,
P. O. Box 40,
Kijabe.

Published by

Zapf Chancery Publishers Africa Ltd,
C/O St. Paul's University
P. O. Box Private Bag,
Limuru - 00217, Kenya.
Email: info@zapfchancery.org
Our Website: www.zapfchancery.org
Mobile: 0721-222 311

ISBN 978-9966-1506-9-1

This book has been printed on fully recyclable, environment-friendly paper.

TO THE COMMUNITY OF MY HEART
my family, friends, students and
all beloved sojourners in faith

Soli Deo Gloria

Acknowledgements

All the chapters in this book, although they have not appeared in print elsewhere, originated from papers that were presented at various conferences. In the process of revising them for the purpose of this book, I enormously benefitted from comments by participants who were the first audience and peer-services during the conferences at which the papers were presented.

Chapter One is based on a paper initially presented at a symposium on Christianity and Ethnicity organized by St. Paul's University in May 2010. Chapter Two was presented at a FOCUS consultation on mission during their inaugural lecturers of the Institute for Mission Dialogue in February 2010. Chapter three is a revised version of a paper presented at the consultation of the Protestant Institution on Theological Education in East Africa organized by the Faculty of Protestant Theology and Religious Studies of the Protestant Institute of Arts and Social Sciences in Butare, Rwanda in May 2010. Chapter four is a revision of a paper presented at a symposium of Theology and Society, Nairobi in October 2005, which in turn, was the revised version of a paper published as, 'Impact of Pentecostalism on the Mainline Churches in Kenya," in a Journal: *Encounter* 1.3 (2003), pp.28-41.

I am grateful to those whose invitations first afforded the opportunity to research on the topics that have here evolved into these chapters. Many colleagues and friends read part or whole of these chapters. I am particularly indebted to my colleague and teacher the Rev. Dr. Sammy Githuku for his valuable comments on chapter one, and the Rev. C.B. Peter for reading and editing the entire book. I must express my profound gratitude to Dr. Timothy Wachira, who graciously agreed to read and write a foreword for this work. I am also very grateful to all my theology students whose critical search for knowledge and theological conversations, in and out of class, have continued to sharpen my thoughts on matters of God and life.

I also acknowledge the abundant joy I have in the grace of God as well as the love and support of my family. To all, I say thank you! To God be the glory!

Foreword

The title of this book is rather surprising. How can Christianity in Africa be referred to as 'stranger' to a people with whom it has interacted for over a century? How can it be described as 'foreign' in a continent where the Church is most vibrant and with a legendry growth rate? As if this claim is not astonishing enough, professor Galgalo in chapter one goes further to declare that if hope for an authentic African Christianity were to be realized, what we now know as African Christianity must first die!

This book, however, is quite readable and engaging. Professor Galgalo gives us a very helpful critical analysis of Christianity in Africa from historical, theological and sociological perspectives. This he ably does both as an academic theologian and as an African Christian who has observed and lived through the religious life in Africa. Students of theology at university level will find this book a very helpful aid while seeking to undertake studies in missiology especially as it relates to the themes of church planting, the gospel and culture, and the integral nature of the mission of the Church. The author's thesis is that theology that is taught and learnt in a conversational mode, and is God centered, bears fruit for living and spiritual growth, especially in as far as it bears on the sources of theology, shapes a contextual hermeneutic and aids a deep theological reflection that is thoroughly contextual and at the same time truly biblical.

Professor Galgalo has made every effort to steer away from theological jargons. The book is therefore accessible to non-theologians. I highly commend it to all interested in the health of the

Church in Africa. To the African Church, the book is an excellent mirror. In a very candid way, the author exposes the two-faced nature of the African Church. I have greatly appreciated the manner in which he has done this. It is quite clear that this is the Church he loves. A Church he longs to see transformed more and more into a truly African authentic Church that is faithful to its calling within its context. The author finally is able to see the strength of African Christianity and make several practical recommendations with a hope that an African Church that "brings about abundance of life that the Gospel promises" can be realized.

Dr. Timothy Wachira
Vice Chancellor, Daystar University

Contents

Acknowledgements	vii
Foreword	ix
Introduction	1
Chapter One: African Christianity: The Stranger Within	4
Introduction	4
Christian but …	4
Historical Origins: An Overview	7
The Pitfalls of Missionary Christianity	12
Why did Africans accept Christianity in the first place?	18
African Christianity: 'the stranger within'	23
Conclusion	29
Chapter Two: Mission	31
Introduction	31
A Different way of doing Mission	31
Mission begins with self	33
Mission is *missio Dei*, not *missio homo*	36
Christianity as we know it must die, that faith may live	41
Mission is not about power, but about charisma	44
Conclusion: Re-thinking Mission	47
Chapter Three: Theological Education	49
Introduction	49

African Christianity: Phenomenal Numerical Strength	49
A Good Theological Education is needed for a Good theology	52
Models of Theological Education in Africa	54
Structural Models	56
The *Academic or Curricular* Model	60
The Hermeneutical Model	63
What is the future of Western theological Models in the African context?	65
Contextualization: Theology for God's People	65
The Doctrine of God: A Sketch	68
Conclusion	71
Chapter Four: African Christianity: Prospects and New Directions	73
Introduction	73
Is Christianity too heavenly oriented and largely irrelevant for life here and now?	73
Images of Jesus	76
Pentecostalism: The Christianity of the Future?	80
Heavenly Vision for Earthly Glory: The 'faith-gospel' Doctrine	82
Faith Gospel and its implications for Eschatology	91
Future Directions: "Nothing Sells Like God"	95
Conclusion: *Quo Vadis*?	97
Chapter Five: Towards A Conversational Model	99
Introduction	99
A Conversational Model	99
The Gospel in Conversation with the Context	101
The Academy in Conversation with the Church	102
An Inter-Church Conversation	104
Conclusion	105

Chapter Six: Conclusion	107
Bibliography	109
Index	115

Introduction

There are books that need to be re-written almost as soon as their first draft is finished. This little book is one such book. It is about the church in Africa, its mission, theology, future and the state of our Christianity. The church is in a constant flux, changing with changing times. This is partly due to the need to stay relevant and partly due to pressures and influences that constantly shape and re-shape the church, not forgetting the possibilities of occasionally being knocked out of shape. In any case, the church—as an organic reality that is growing towards full maturity—is on its way to becoming that which it ought to become. That growth being its nature, change is anyway, inevitable.

Christianity in Africa is vibrant and pervasive. Churches are rapidly being established although may be not as securely as it could be. Christianity is increasingly becoming a way of life for most Africans in the regions of East, Central, South and West Africa. While leading scholars of Christian missions positively assess Africa's embrace of Christianity, seeing the African church as the church of the future, a few critics, though equally perceptive are not as confident. The depth and authenticity of African Christianity have come under sharp scrutiny; that Christianity may be everywhere in Africa but is yet to take deep and meaningful roots as it should. Some of the major criticisms often leveled against African Christianity are the shallowness of theology, syncretism and faith-claims that contradict actual practical living.

It is such shallowness and contradictions that have earned African Christianity the reputation of superficiality at best, and at worst, blatant hypocrisy or double allegiance of sorts. Some have come to the radical conclusion that the church in Africa has lost the gospel altogether and has built systems and institutions on ethnic bedrocks, and characteristically specialized in legalism, moralism and money matters – busy extorting members, with regard to this last point, if not extending the begging bowl to the West.

This little book probes to some extent concerns about African Christianity. The scope is intentionally limited for good and obvious reasons. Even when 'Africa' is used in a rather generic sense, Kenya is particularly borne in mind. This latter context provides us with our focus and illustrations. We basically raise four questions regarding the church in Africa. The first two questions are on the nature and mission of the Church. We start by probing the depth and authenticity of African Christianity and ask: 'What makes African Christianity Christian?' And follow this with: 'what is the mission of the African church?' The last two questions are on the theology and future of the church in Africa. It is here that we ask: 'What is the theology of the African church?' and follow this up with, 'What is the future of the Church in Africa or more precisely of African Christianity?' It must be pointed out that these questions are theologically of preliminary nature and the answers are only tentative; not least because of the general nature of this work but also because of the dynamic nature of the reality of the church and fluidity of the context in which we live.

Marginality in matters of faith and nominal tendencies has ironically become a banner of comfort for the truly faithful, not least because these have become acceptable marks of the church. Comfort is taken in the words of Jesus that after all 'many are called, but only a few are chosen,' and that the church is like a field of wheat interspersed with weeds, and that it is after all biblical to let the wheat and tare grow together. We do not pretend that the church is not a communion of saints and sinners all at the same time; yet we do not hesitate to raise the bar with regard to the question of faithfulness to the very foundation of faith itself and of the demands that this puts upon us. Right doctrine and praxis, that should rightly inform each other, are here uppermost in my mind.

The problem with the church today is that numerical strength is erroneously used as the criteria for measuring the effectiveness of the church's task in discipleship and mission. The quest for membership has largely produced a Christianity of convenience, where members take on faith as a role play and where rehearsed formula such as 'I am saved' has become the sole determinant for inclusion or exclusion into a given status, recognition or social belonging. The result is an abundance of the presence of a Christianity that is followed by all yet upheld by only a few. There is a pervasive and contagious confession of faith yet without the evidence of its power to change lives or transform communities of faith. The onus is on us to show, in the next few short chapters, whether this claim is valid.

CHAPTER ONE

African Christianity: The Stranger Within

Introduction

There is a paradox at the heart of African Christianity. It is vibrant and growing but at the same time shallow and superficial. It struggles with nominalism, syncreticism, increasing secularism, and the ever changing social and political realities and the challenges of relevance that come with such changes. The present chapter probes probable historical reasons perceived to be largely responsible for the present state of African Christianity. To help us address this paradox, we propose two possible solutions: a rethinking of mission and strengthening of theological education, but these two are addressed in chapter two and three respectively. Let us first dispense with the question of the existing paradox.

Christian but ...

What makes African Christianity *Christian*? Is the distinction often made between 'African Christians' on the one hand and 'Christian Africans' on the other valid? In whatever ways one looks at it, the two expressions seem to carry different connotations. The debate over the question of 'African-Christian' vis-à-vis 'Christian-African,' draws out varied understandings and interpretations, and of course implications and emphases that arise with differences in views. A common way of looking at this debate is to use the yardstick of loyalty as the hermeneutical key to help distinguish between committed Christians and common nominal Christians; or the wheat from the tare, as the New Testament puts it. When an 'African Christian' is faced by a cultural-religious demand that conflicts with Christian teaching, which of the two, most of the time will take priority over the other? Put differently, are 'African Christians' first Africans and then Christians or just Christians, who also happen to be Africans? A simple observation reveals that the African person lives in a world referenced at every point by religious meaning, where every happening finds a spiritual explanation. It is puzzling that although Christianity is widely followed, yet it often comes a poor second to the African Traditional Religion—at least with regard to being a source for providing such explanations even spiritual anchor or solid reference point.

The adherence to the African traditional beliefs and practices are still very strong among African Christians. When encountering an African, who is already 'religious,' in own way, Christianity often finds a superficial acceptance and comfortably (to great amazement) stands alongside other religious views and cherished beliefs. It is only when conflicts or competition of sorts arise, that we can tell with certainty where true loyalty of the African adherent lies. In Africa, Christianity is for most part a religion of convenience, social identity, a way to be, and not necessarily a spiritual home and certainly not the only spiritual home for most professing Christians. It is true that most African Christians would, as Benezet Bujo observes, "Return to the traditional practices for comfort in times of crisis,"[1] and we may add, that they do so to find spiritual security and meaning in traditional religious beliefs and practices.

It is little wonder then why Christianity often takes a back seat during such times as funerals and the elaborate African rites and rituals that accompany it. The resilience of such traditional practices as upholding ethnic loyalty and identity, fear of magic, practice of witchcraft, resilient polygamy, concubinage, wife inheritance, widow

---

[1]*African Theology in its Social Context*, 1992:31.

cleansing, sexual taboos, female initiation and burial rites[2] is evidence that the African Christian still largely operates in the African traditional religious mind-set. As Allan Anderson perceptively describes, "These burial and mourning customs [and such other African religious beliefs and practices] suggest that many practices still prevailing in African Christianity ... are vestiges of [African traditional religion and that] ... the church does not always determine the form of the funeral."[3] We have welcomed and accepted Christianity even though it largely remains a stranger of sorts in the midst of the African traditional and religious world.

My conceptual framework is that African Christianity, planted in Africa in the context of colonialism and oppression, has only managed to effect a social adjustment of sorts. At a deeper level, Christianity has failed to inspire, reshape or transform African social history and basic identity. A glance through history may unravel why Christianity even though widely accepted and followed in Africa yet has remained a stranger within the phenomenal world of African religiosity.

Historical Origins: An Overview

Africa boasts a long Christian history, which may be reviewed in three parts. The first part pertains to the classical period of church history in North Africa. The Gospel according to Matthew shows that Christ was in Africa long before Christianity was known or followed by anyone. The ancient church in Egypt cherished the tradition that the Savior of the world was at one time a refugee in

---

[2]Most African communities practice elaborate burial ceremonies and conduct prescribed rituals in accordance with age old beliefs, taboos, obligations and expectations placed upon the living relatives of the deceased by the society. Some of the commonest practices include: set period of mourning; 'appeasing' the spirit of the dead, cleansing rituals (often involving sacrifices to wade off evil spirits), disposal or distribution of the property or personal belongings of the deceased, etc.

[3]http://deathreference.com/A-B:/African-Religions.html, October 2011.

their land. Historical and Biblical accounts testify to Christianity's contact with Africa from very early times—perhaps as early as the beginning of Christianity itself. The book of Acts (2:9-11) mentions Egyptians, Libyans and Cyreneans, among the crowd that heard the first Pentecost sermon. If there are possibilities that some may have been converted and if they took their new found faith home, then Christianity may have taken root in their parts of Africa right from the beginning of the earliest Christian movement. Acts 8:26-40 tells the story of the eunuch, an official of the Candice who believed in Christ after an encounter with Philip the Apostle. If this official used his influence to convert others to his faith, we can make a reasonable guess that a Christian congregation may have been established in his part of Africa from very early on. The book of Acts (11:20) also makes an important assertion that Christians from Cyrene were involved in active leadership of the church of Antioch. We also know from Acts 18:24-28 that Apollos the Christian philosopher, and a key itinerant preacher who got converted while on a visit to Ephesus was from Egypt. It is possible that Apollos may have had a hand in establishing churches in his native land.

These possibilities aside, there are historical accounts that affirm the presence of Christianity in Africa from the earliest period of Christianity's beginnings. Early Christian tradition has it that the church in Alexandria was established through the missionary activity of St. Mark the gospel writer.[4] In any case North Africa, Numidia, Nubia, Abyssinia and Egypt were home to Christianity right from the first century of the Christian era. Indeed most of these parts were evangelized most likely long before Europe ever heard of the Gospel. John Parratt observes that in the early days of Christianity:

---

[4]Eusebius of Caesarea, the author of *Ecclesiastical History* in the 4th century, states that St. Mark came to Egypt in the first or third year of the reign of Emperor Claudius, which was early Forties (about 41 to 43 A.D.) *Two Thousand Years of Coptic Christianity*, Otto F.A. Meinardus, 28.

Christian Africa looked across at pagan Europe and for centuries it was Africa that was the seedbed of Christian theology. Towards the end of second century the North African church entered the light of Christian history with thinkers such as Tertullian, Cyprian, and Augustine, while to the East Egypt produced its Origen, Clement, and Athanasius. Most of our Christian doctrines were formulated by these early African theologians, and, one might argue, most of the early heresies had their origins here too.[5]

This early Christianity never reached down to 'Black Africa' but remained an essentially a Mediterranean affair. Little was known of the rest of Africa at this time. The Christianity of Egypt and North Africa that flourished for over 600 years, reached its climax, waned and died a gradual death under massive Arabization and islamization of these regions, and not least due to internal Christian conflicts, schisms and heresies, which greatly weakened the Church. The tiny bastions that are now left constantly struggle under Islamic domination and suffer acute isolation, largely cut off from the rest of the Christian world. In any case, the first phase of Christianity in Africa cannot be claimed for the whole of Africa for the simple reason that its influence outside its own confines to northern regions is indeed non-existent.

The second phase of Christianity in Africa goes back to the 15th century. It is associated with the coming of the Portuguese who colonized parts of East Coast of Africa, West Coast and Central parts of Africa. The Portuguese missionary activities concentrated mainly in the regions today called the Democratic Republic of Congo and areas that today form parts of Angola. The resultant Portuguese-African Christianity, which was planted in the context of subjugation and exploitation of the conquered peoples, lasted only for about 200 years. The Bakongo Christianity did not survive for long after the end of the Portuguese rule. It is puzzling that the Bakongo Christians

---

[5]*Reinventing Christianity: African Theology Today*, (Williams B Eerdmans Publishing Company, Grand Rapids, Michigan/Cambridge, UK, 1995), 3.

gradually abandoned all Christian practices including such key Christian rituals as baptism, the Lord's Supper and regular worship meetings. The only lasting legacy of what was once a vibrant Christianity was perhaps a few references to Portuguese names (adopted once as 'Christian' or baptismal names), relics (bits and pieces of crucifix or ruins of what once were church buildings. The reasons for such turn of affairs are rather intriguing. Just to highlight one example, the Portuguese began the evangelization of the Bakongo Kingdom, in the heart of Africa, from 1491. A strong church was established not through mass conversions but a steady stream of catechumens who were thoroughly taught in the way of Christ before they were baptized.

Over the next 150 years or so, Christianity in the Congo steadily grew. From 1650 onwards, the evangelization of the Congo was mainly spearheaded by the Capuchins, an offshoot of the Franciscans order. In the period between 1645 and 1835 about 440 friars, mainly of the Capuchin Mission labored in the Congo but mainly in the region today called Angola. A great number of Africans accepted Christianity and became the followers. As early as 1556 a Portuguese catechism was available in the Bakongo language; becoming the first literature ever to have been produced in the Bantu language. Although the Congo Christianity flourished for a good long time, it waned and finally died, almost leaving no significant traces of its once vibrant existence. It is simply baffling how this could happen after such a seemingly solid foundation. Talking of foundation—that is exactly the problem; far from being solid, there was no much of a foundation to begin with. In the circumstances, the fall is obvious and even expected. Sundkler and Steed sketch a graphic picture of this phase of African Christianity's demise. They are precisely spots on regarding the reason for such turn of events:

> During the 18th century the Congo church slowly but inevitably faded away and in the end only a few sad traces and ruins remained, leaving the impression that it had perhaps throughout been nothing

but an illusion ... and never more than a thin veneer over a groundwork of solid traditional religion.[6]

The East Coast experience was equally such an unhappy affair where the resentment towards the *Wareno* (as the Portuguese were referred to in this region) may have had a lot to do with the peoples' rejection of Christianity and the subsequent mass conversions to Islam. I contend that learning from history is fruitful for a perceptive assessment of the true nature of present day African Christianity as well as discerning the future directions of the African Church. Judging by the pattern of the first two phases of African Christianity, it will not surprise me in the least if the circle of the birth, death and rebirth of African Christianity proves true for all other phases of African Christianity.

The third phase, which is the present phase of African Christianity, is now about 200 years old. This phase of Christianity was mainly established from the 19th century onwards through the work of European and American missionaries. Once again, as was the case with the second phase (and to some extent the first phase), Christianity of the third phase also was established in the context of colonialism and Western imperialism. Even the missionary work in Sierra Leone, the place where the story of the third phase begins, was for a long time controlled by America and England, founded initially as a home for freed slaves; Sierra Leone was eventually colonized by the British until 1961.

The formation of numerous mission societies from around the close of 18th century saw massive evangelization of most parts of Africa. Although mission boards operated independently of their home governments, the planting of churches in Africa went hand in hand with the political conquest of Africa, where the Flag often paved the way for the bible or the Bible preceded and invited the Flag to establish control in the heartlands of Africa and provide security for the missionaries.

---

[6]Ibid, 55.

The Pitfalls of Missionary Christianity

Although the church in Africa presently seems to be firmly established, it cannot be argued with much confidence that missionaries this time round laid a better foundation than was the case with the earlier phases of Christianity in Africa. It is remarkable that today a good many congregations and denominations throughout Africa are locally founded. They have evolved independent of Western missionary influences, and some are even unheard of in the West. As history has proved twice over already, but more so going by plenty of signs already at hand, it is likely that the present day vibrant Christianity may have seen its better days and could be only a matter of time before it goes the way of the African Christianity of the earlier phases. The fact of its shaky foundation is not in doubt. The missionary methods were in most places questionable and the kind of Christianity they planted, for most part, received a rather unstable grounding, and besides reasons of faith, Christianity was 'received' for a host of other reasons. Once again, it is a repeat of a story that now is only too familiar; of a Christianity that is but a "thin veneer over a groundwork of solid traditional religion."

However, it is likely but maybe not possible that Christianity this time round may simply die out. There are emerging trends and new directions that may sustain Christian following well into the future as we shall see in chapter four below. What most likely may happen is what C.B. Peter called, 'the African hyphenated Christians,' who will provide an "alternate model of theologizing in Africa," and shape the emergence of a distinctive 'African Christianity.' As C. B. Peter contends, African Christianity will emerge as a confluence of two major influences: the Bible (and the Judeo-Christian tradition) on the one hand, and the African traditional religion and cultures on the other. It is likely that, the mixture of these two influences will determine the shape, practices and core beliefs of what will emerge and remain as 'African Christianity.'[7]

---

[7] C. B. Peter, "African Hyphenated Christians – An Alternate Model of Theologizing in Africa," in *Nordic Journal of African Studies* 3(1), 1994.

Western missionaries planted churches in Africa on the model of their home churches. Western ways of evangelism, forms of Christianity and mission strategies were replete with many shortcomings. The first major pitfall is the colonial context in which Christianity was planted in Africa. Colonialism, the context in which Christianity was spread, was rather a curse than a blessing. Most missionaries, of course, regarded it as divine providence that the colonial governments provided security and helped them to access places that otherwise they would not have reached. But the flip side of this blessing meant the seed of the gospel was sown in the soil of mistrust and suspicion, especially where white missionaries were identified with the much resented colonial power. Missionaries were in some cases direct agents of the colonial governments and did little to exonerate themselves from the accusations that they were collaborators with the oppressive colonial powers. It also did not help matters that some missionaries freely and openly used the colonial influence, protection and patronage to coerce Africans for the furtherance of their missionary work. This produced a Christianity of social and political convenience where many joined, or even today belong to a church, not truly out of faith and genuine commitment but out of historical circumstances, the need for cooperation, affiliation, vested interest or incidental belonging such as through marriage or filial relations.

The other pitfall of the missionary Christianity was that the missionaries imposed upon African converts their Western denominational brands of Christianity. For the foreign missionaries, mission was about institutional expansion and the propagation of their sectarian, denominational Christianity. This unfortunate approach divided African communities into religious groupings hitherto somewhat alien to African peoples. It was unheard of, for example, that members of the same family or clan could worship separately and conduct their religious affairs in exclusion of one another. One obvious result of such religious or denominational divisions was the African perception of the church as a political and social force where control of a denominational turf becomes a means to power and domination. Missionary Christianity sowed the seed for a new political dimension of religion in Africa. It is no wonder that the early splinter groups and 'new churches' were almost always caused by leadership wrangles and power struggles and hardly ever about more important matters such as doctrinal differences. As a result, African Christianity to date is often not so much about faith, truth and service but about power, position and status.

The third major pitfall was perhaps African Christianity's major undoing. Most missionaries, to give credit where it is due, did their best within the limit of their abilities to learn African customs and languages; and applied what in their best judgment they deemed as the best approach in the prevailing circumstances. Unfortunately such missionaries were very few. The majority did little or nothing at all to understand African cultures, customs and religious practices. On the contrary, driven by the zeal and conviction to redeem Africa's 'dark cultures,' they saw their mission primarily as that of uprooting 'heathenism' and planting Christianity. This explains why everything African was seen as barbaric and ungodly and were usually condemned wholesale.

Most of the earlier missionaries operated from a theological framework that advocated total conversion of the African person from perceived heathenism to Christianity. Although, this was done with the best of intentions, it involved uncritical assumption that the African person religiously speaking is 'an empty vessel', ready to be filled with Christian content. However, since the Gospel encounters the African person from a particular religious vantage point, it will make sense if the traditional religious experience of the Africans can be considered as a useful foregrounding to communicate the new religious truth.

It should also not be forgotten that the Gospel, after all, offers both universal and unique truths. In many cases, the Gospel only highlights the truth, which we knew all along. The Gospel recasts such truth for us in fresh and new ways thereby clarifying and purifying it. Today, as a result of the missionaries 'empty and refill' or 'uproot and plant' method, we have Christians who are still strongly rooted in their cultural beliefs or are at best, simply confused – partaking of both of these religions and overlooking even apparent contradictions. These Christians, having received Christianity as a second home alongside their traditional spirituality, constantly move between these two religious homes, each complete with its thought-world, beliefs and practices – borrowing and applying elements from both as it suits them. This explains, to use an idea that was first coined by Bishop Desmond Tutu, why African Christianity suffers from such an acute spiritual schizophrenia.

Another pitfall that needs to be mentioned is the general missionary attitude and culture. The Enlightenment culture of Europe was, for most part, the cultural paradigm within which the missionaries operated. A key Enlightenment cultural value is the belief in the power of reason, human intellect and progress. The missionaries generally saw African cultures as rudimentary and lacking in philosophical sophistication. This coupled with the fact that African cultures were generally unlettered reinforced their belief that Africans were intellectually inferior. For most of these missionaries Darwinism and generally some forms of evolutionary theories provided them with their basic philosophical framework.

The resultant imperialism and racial superiority complex was a direct contradiction to the Gospel of love and equality. The Kenyan context provides an apt example where the 'white' missionary was always the *bwana* (master) and the 'convert' employee, is 'the *boy,*' (servant) a far cry from being a brother or sister in Christ as it should have been. The practice of master and servant distinctions created perceptions of a casted Christianity; where acceptance into a particular church received connotations of acceptance into the supposedly 'superior' white caste. This practice and the attitude that went with it may have changed with missionaries of the more recent or later years but the unfortunate legacy and the residual cultural view lingers on. A good many Africans would today see the church, particularly of the churches that are of missionary origins, as a church of a particular class of people, far from being a spiritual home for all believers. It is interesting to observe that most new church movements, especially those in urban settings, tend to foster a system of social class, where people of similar income levels, educational background and age tend to congregate.

Finally, the missionaries' widespread culture of paternalism undermined the development of African church leadership. After African countries begun gaining political independence from the colonialists, there still remained a deliberate attitude to keep the church under 'mission' control for as long as possible. This became a source of distrust, rivalry and bad blood. The rise of nationalism inspired the movement for the liberation of the African from 'mission' domination and tutelage not only in the public political arena but also in the church. Within the church circles, the climax of this movement was in the moratorium debate. The moratorium debate was initiated in the 1970s by Africans who felt frustrated by what they saw as a slow transition of African Christianity from mission to church especially with regard to the Africanization of the church leadership. The debate was mainly revolved around the question of whether the church in politically independent Africa still needed Western missionaries. Anti-missionary sentiment was particularly strong among the Protestant church adherents for whom the moratorium was about the African churches' rejection of European personnel and financial resources that was argued to perpetuate dominance on one hand, and dependency on the other. It was a call for the missionaries to withdraw and allow the African churches to develop their own resources and manage their own programs. The debate reached a climax when a motion to place a moratorium on mission funding and personnel was adopted by the third assembly of AACC sitting in Lusaka in May 1974. The proceedings generated further debate when it was published and no commentator was perhaps as radical as Fabien Boulaga who lent his support in the words: "let Europe and America give priority to their own evangelization. Let us plan the orderly departure of missionaries from Africa."[8]

The Moratorium debate generated a process that led to the desired results but also produced some unforeseen side effects which were not quite as pleasant. First of all, it ignored the fact of mutuality and interdependency of the universal church of Christ. The urgency of the debate, and the realities of the changing times in the post-independent Africa placed white controlled churches under pressure to heed the call for the Africanization of the African church. Ill prepared, the missionary churches, particularly of the Protestant orientations, generally did a shoddy job of handing over the leadership of the churches to the Africans. They generally lacked exit strategy, readiness, adequate time and a systematic plan that such transition required.

Consequently, two things may be notes as particularly regrettable. First, the missionaries handpicked ordinands to fill the huge need for personnel. Patronage, ability to read and write, and active membership in the church became the criteria for selecting those who got trained, and eventually ordained for church leadership. Most of such handpicked leaders lacked the necessary calling and acumen but had to fit in, thanks to the coaching by their mentors. Faith and the requisite calling for holy orders became natural affirmations not that they may be genuine but became handy in order to be seen to fulfill the demands of the job description. In most cases, trainings too were hasty and inadequate. This slowly but firmly ended by placing church leadership in the hands of largely unqualified personnel. The current state of the church characterized by lack of vision, quality service, relevant structures, mission strategies and weak theology is a direct fruit of the seeds of the mismanaged transition and poor foundation. Evidence of this sad state of affairs is all around us. Poor leadership, mismanagement, widespread

---

[8]Boulaga Fabien Eboussi, 1974, "La demission," in *Spiritus*, vol.56, 276-287.

nepotism and ethnicity are a general hallmark of most churches in Africa today.

Second, since the Church was ill-prepared to support its programs, and since the missionaries largely determined or hand-picked their successors, they had huge influence on the succession process and were able to perpetuate the culture of patronage. The continuing effect of this is the current tendency of the African church to continue looking to the West for guidance and support, especially in the areas of theological education, social programs and financial aid. In a sense, the African Church is still a 'mission church' and is run, albeit from a distance, by the mother church in the West.

It was against such background that Christianity took root in Africa and to date struggles with the effects of some of the ills of missionary legacy. The Church continues to suffer under the inadequacy of inherited Western church structures, policies, constitutions, orders and theology which, by and large, are ill-fitting for the African context. The church in Africa is yet to read the Bible through its own lenses and find a way to appropriately and effectively plant the gospel message in the African soil and realize the incarnation of the Word in the African cultural setting. In many ways, African Christianity is still so foreign to the African soil, and although Africa has Christianity, Christianity does not have Africa. On this basis we conclude that African Christianity, which is widely confessed, is still a stranger within its true African spiritual home, where it enjoys enormous hospitality but hardly commands meaningful or serious loyalty.

Why Did Africans Accept Christianity in the First Place?
We cannot doubt that faith has drawn many Africans to Christ, but we also acknowledge that Christianity means different things to its different followers. For many, faith or practical demands of faith may not matter that much, so long as they can 'simply belong' or identify with the Church for all sorts of reasons. An analysis of historical background to the present African Christianity helpfully reveals the reasons why there are Christians who simply choose to

belong but without bothering to follow it up with faith-commitment. We simply need to look at how early missionaries presented Christianity to Africa and we can discover various reasons why in the first place Africans were at all attracted to 'colonial Christianity.'

It should not be overlooked that African communities had their own forms of spirituality and elaborate religious systems. God was no stranger to Africa and needed no introduction. Most African communities believed and worshipped a universal God, and although recognizing the existence of only one God, they also acknowledged that different tribes had different ways of worship and a means of access to God, a way that was unique to each ethnic group. There was a clear monotheism, which nevertheless closely bordered on henotheism. Christianity reinforced the belief in one universal God but in addition promised an entry into a wider Christian family that would transcend ethnic boundaries and embrace the entire human race. The promise of the new religion to create wider and lager communities was attractive, not least for among other things, broadened sense of security and solidarity that was helpful for reference in times of social and spiritual difficulties.

Seen in this light, Christianity also presented the promise to create unity in bringing together warring communities and help them overcome ethnic animosity. This was particularly significant for those communities that endured constant attacks and longed for peace and harmonious co-existence with their aggressive neighbors. Unfortunately time has now proved that actualizing Christianity's potential as the religion of peace and brotherhood has remained elusive. Africans are still deeply entrenched in their own distinct cultures where individual identities are primarily determined by ethnic membership, family ties and cultural backgrounds. Consequently, an African Christian's loyalty is always first and foremost to the tribe (through extended network of families, relatives and clan) and only secondly to the wider Christian family. A good example is the Kenyan situation. The perennial ethnic clashes in Kenya often pities one ethnic group against another—their belonging together, as members of the same church, notwithstanding. The point we are making is that whereas Christianity has a great potential as a unifier of believers from across cultural, ethnic and social divides, and whereas this very fact was a source of attraction to Christianity for some African communities, this potential, generally speaking, has not been achieved and conflict often pits one Christian group against another, who are divided along ethnic lines.

There were also social, psychological and religious factors that influenced the Africans' embrace of Christianity. Slave trade left an indelible mark on the African psyche. In the context of the brutal trade, "Jesus was misused and betrayed—and still somehow "transmitted."[9] What an irony that the faith of the slave masters and merchants in 'human cargo' would at all appeal to the victims of that very slave trade! J.G. Haafner wonders how in the face of the disgrace of slavery anyone would "accept the God of those who exercised tyranny over them."[10] Indeed it is puzzling as Vincent Harding observes that, "although many black men have rejected this Christ—indeed the miracle is that so many accepted him."[11] Christianity was perhaps accepted, as many would argue, not least as a palliative and the only anchor under the cruelty of such proportion. But more likely, as the Africans reflected on their relationship with Jesus in the light of their faith experience, they must have distanced Jesus from their 'Christian' oppressors. Christ, if not Christianity was accepted mainly because of the attractive message that preached dignity and value of all human beings, a vision of inclusive humanity, individual freedom, human rights, justice, equality and honor. In the circumstances, it is not difficult to tell why these poor Africans, thirsty and hungry for these values were attracted to Jesus who promised all these and even more. It is then not surprising that many accepted Christ and genuinely so.

---

[9]Anton Wessels, *Images of Jesus: How Jesus is Perceived and Portrayed in Non-European Cultures* (London: SCM, 1990), 84-85.
[10]Ibid, 86-87 .
[11]Cited in ibid, 207.

Similarly, Christ was received in Africa, at the hands of missionaries whose lives and Christian integrity often were a far cry from that of Christ and his message that they preached. The message of Christ, if only for its inspirational power, easily found a soft touch among the poor, the captives and the lowly—categories that applied to majority of the African masses. Due to the hierarchical nature of relationships within most African societies, there were often those who found themselves on the margins of the mainstream of their societies. The downtrodden and the oppressed must have found hope and promising solutions to their cry for affirmation of their basic inalienable human rights. Indeed in the beginning, the bulk of the African converts were fugitives, social misfits or outcasts, ex-slaves and the destitute, who in becoming Christian found new identities.[12] In Christ, they could discard the old identities and embraced new beginnings as 'new creation in Christ.' Many, even today, take on the Christian label to forge new identities or the directions in life all in effort to shed off unwanted baggage. This explains why some would constantly move from one church to another in search of a sense of recognition, belonging to, and social acceptance and psychological satisfaction. The constant shift of allegiance from one group to another is an indication that their 'conversion' is not to Christianity *per se* or religious as such, but sociological, where belonging to a 'new social group' could afford 'new identity.'

At a totally different level, missionary Christianity was also accepted for its philosophical attractiveness. The intellectual content of the Christian teaching of God came to be regarded by some Africans as more dignified, more appealing, and satisfying than the traditional teaching about deities. Seen as philosophically superior, and associated with missionary schools that provided new forms of education and introduced new centers of learning, Christianity came to be seen as the religion of the 'civilized' and the outward mark of

---

[12]For a great exposition of this, see J. K. Karanja, *Founding an African Faith: Kikuyu Anglican Christianity, 1900 – 1945* (Nairobi: Uzima Press, 1999).

the *wasomi* (scholars).[13] This meant that Christianity was simply part of the package where schooling was not necessarily separated from church attendance and participating in the rituals that went with it. Credible belief and serious commitment to Christian teachings or faith was not necessarily the reason for the much celebrated mass conversions. Christianity became the 'normal' way to be, but its system and teachings did not automatically provide the norm. This scenario provides the backdrop to the present situation where majority of African Christians happily uphold the outward performances of Christian rituals such as sacraments, church weddings, Sunday worship and festive observances even when they may not believe or take seriously all the demands of biblical teachings. There are also many who join or remain in the church for reasons such as being born in it, brought up in it or married into it, as are those who join or remain members on account of faith alone.

Another reason why most Africans embraced Christianity was the motivation to enhance one's social status and especially to gain an opportunity for social mobility. In this sense, Christianity was seen, not so much as a religion that taught a special way to God, but as a way that afforded special opportunities, a real tool or a means to an end. Christianity, with its emphasis on Western education—all intended for the Africans to read the Bible for themselves, proved providential when literacy also became part of the qualification for gainful employment, leadership and status. This laid the foundation for opportunistic tendencies that, generally, never hesitate to appropriate Christianity for itself if such exploit may afford a means to a desired end.

Closely related to what we have already said, Africans also accepted missionary Christianity for the love of western education. Missionary Christianity and its culture attracted and even enticed Africans by its literacy and book learning. The Western way of learning and literacy carried something of a magical aura. We could

---

[13]See, J. K. Karanja, *Founding an African Faith: Kikuyu Anglican Christianity, 1900 – 1945* (Nairobi: Uzima Press, 1999).

imagine creations and recreations of various impressions, appearances, and imaginations, and the effects produced by the ability to externally preserve memory, keep accurate records and document knowledge, in view of the then predominantly non-literate African societies who were experiencing this magic and power of literacy for the first time. Much of the fascination is still present although for totally different reasons. African Christianity keeps evolving in different ways and the particular brands that today fascinate its followers and hold them captive are those that promise the miracles of healing, wealth and power. It is the type of Simon Magus curiosity and the desire to receive access to 'powers from beyond' that attracts many to these churches. Ironically, faith is thereby received or confession of it accepted as the requisite key to achieving the desired goal.

The foregoing analysis shows that faith was only one reason among many why Africans embraced Christianity. The fear is that the numerical growth of African Christianity may simply be like a bubble without much content. Seeing the kind of a somewhat shaky foundation on which African Christianity is built, the common criticism that African Christianity is like a shallow river, a few inches deep and miles wide may not easily be rebuffed. Now that the reasons that initially attracted Africans to Christianity are increasingly becoming irrelevant or largely replaced, it is likely that secularism or more likely the resurgence of African traditional religions will slowly bring about the demise of the current phase of African Christianity. We shall briefly return to the question of why Africans are still attracted to Christianity; but first, why has Christianity remained a stranger for such a long time in the African spiritual home? To these questions, we now turn.

African Christianity: 'The Stranger Within'

Historical provenance has largely contributed to the fact that African Christianity to date lives as a welcomed stranger in the African spiritual home, whose centerpiece is the African traditional religion, and for which Christianity is only a thin veneer, a sort of cover page and not really the content. Africans are today victims of their own social history where the common social feature is of violence, indignity, diseases and troublesome marginal identities like tribalism, neocolonialism and nepotism. Christianity, which if correctly planted, would have had the power and capacity of inspiring a better and alternative vision of society, has sadly become part of the general topology. In the opening sentence of this chapter, we asked, 'what makes African Christianity Christian? And now we come round to attempting an answer to this pertinent question, although in the interest of brevity, we shall provide only a bare outline.

Most African Christians are deeply connected with Christ and at the same time are at a distance from him. They belong to the church and yet at the same time are marginal and occasionally act and live as complete outsiders, with very little or no concern at all for church matters or teachings. The insider-outsider identities so overlap and blend within African Christianity that an individual is capable, all at the same time, of belonging to both of these entities. The differences that separate the insiders from the outsiders are after all, not often as clear as are the commonness that unites them. The outsiders are often the insiders. The common terms of 'saved' (*wokovu*) and 'not yet saved' (*mkristo wa kawaida*) are indicative of the internal categories but not definitive with regard to the insider-outsider distinctions. Majority of Africans would claim Christianity as their religion, if only because of the strong communal bonds that tie them with their fellow community members. They accept membership of the church by meeting basic requirements like baptism, but clearly remain outsiders while appearing to be on the inside. Such 'Christians' may fulfill some requirements like church weddings if they find them of advantage while the more serious Christian commitments may be put on hold if not convenient. Such members are in this case clearly both insiders and outsiders all at same time.

In the practical sense this means one thing. The average 'African Christian,' generally speaking, lives at the 'spiritual' margins of both Christianity and African traditional religion, partaking of both but claiming only one identity—that of being a Christian. This identity is generally characterized by marginality of faith, wavering commitment, doctrinal indifference, syncretistic tendencies, conflicting loyalties and inconsistencies. Such marginal existence on the borders of the two religions seems to have become the norm. The ensuing contradictions may be understood by taking into account the 'African Christianity's' popular understanding of the meaning of the church—that the church is primarily a social organization and only remotely a theological reality or a spiritual home.

This perception explains why majority of the people join the church on social considerations rather than out of faith or theological conviction. This then means that for the majority of African Christians, Christianity's immediacy, relevancy and meaning is in its sociological role and not so much in its doctrinal correctness or theological truth. For majority of the 'African Christians,' that is what makes African Christianity '*Christian*' where many would not hesitate to see themselves a 'Christian' because they are members. On this account, 'social Christianity' has continued attracting followers in great numbers, yet ironically and indeed inevitably remaining a stranger within the African religious world, as far as its spiritual hold on its followers is concerned.

This conclusion leads us to one other question. How 'Christian' is African Christianity? Doctrinal distinctiveness, ethical and moral teachings, beliefs and practices are the basic marks of any religion. African Christianity definitely carries the 'Christian' label but has a lot of the African traditional religious beliefs and practices in its content. The Bible, catechesis, paraphernalia, liturgies, rites, and Christian terminology such as incarnation, redemption, new birth, resurrection, heaven and hell are used. Despite the domestication and usage of these concepts, conceptual differences between Christian doctrines and traditional understanding abound. The differences often reveal a clear dichotomy and sometimes even contradictions between faith claims and ethical or moral applications. Also, faith or theological imperative often is secondary to any social demand. A common place idea is 'what is right with the community must be right by God.'

The reason for this phenomenon is not difficult to explain. There are numerous conceptual differences that arise with regard to views and understanding of such theological subjects as sin, forgiveness or salvation. The concept of sin, for example, for the majority of African Christians is not so much about falling short of God's will, as it is about breaking a taboo or crossing liminal boundaries, that is, the psychological threshold of consciousness. Usually, a given situation would determine the rightness or wrongness of an action. It is important to emphasis action over against thought here because, for most Africans, thought is understood basically in terms of action and even an action is not necessarily sinful unless it automatically ends up disrupting the general tribal harmony or established relationships.

Such actions as ethnic cleansing (that is, murder of persons from a different tribe), widow's sexual cleansing[14] and culturally sanctioned extra marital sexual relations (as in, for example, helping out an impotent brother or a cousin), are within the liminal boundaries. Going by a recent survey that I did among members of Catholics, Anglicans, Presbyterians and Pentecostal Churches, these practices may have changed their forms or simply gone underground but are by no means abandoned. A recent study by Pew Forum, USA, seems to corroborate this survey. The pew study reveals that:

> in spite of impressive religious [Christian] credentials, strong belief in one God, and in heaven and hell, the survey found that sub-Saharan Africa, Kenya included, leads in the worship of alternative gods—witchcraft, evil spirits, and sacrifices to ancestors,

---

[14]Sexual cleansing is a religious practice common among many African ethnic communities in Zimbabwe, Malawi, Zambia, Mozambique and Kenya. The practice involves subjecting a widow whose husband has just died to a ritual sex with a stranger (someone not known to the widow). In some cases, the widow is required to have intercourse with one of her late husband's close relatives like a cousin or brother. The ritual is believed to protect the widow from her husband's ghost, who otherwise will return to haunt her.

traditional religious healers and reincarnation. Kenya is ranked 15th in Africa in its people's belief in witchcraft, a few points behind the Democratic Republic of Congo, and way ahead of Ethiopia, Nigeria, Zambia and Rwanda. A quarter of Kenyans, both Christians and Muslims, confessed they believe in the protective power of juju (charms or amulets) and that they consult traditional healers. A number admitted to revering their dead ancestors and treasuring animal skins and skulls or knowing of friends or relatives who identify with these faiths.[15]

The main reason for the tenacity of such practices is because they are hardly perceived as sin despite the influence of Christian teaching. On the contrary, disregard for such practices is usually interpreted as a serious breach of a moral duty, such an evil (or sin) that can attract curse, the cause of human misfortunes: including illnesses, barrenness, sudden deaths, miscarriages, loss of property and conflicts. The puzzle of 'why Africans are still attracted to Christianity' here then finds an answer. While for many Africans syncretism typically characterizes their religious beliefs and practices, for many others, Christianity is their social garb; and traditional religion their natural spiritual home. The theological framework that sustains this dual belonging is rather subtle: All religious beliefs and practices are a means to an end—and whatever works in fulfilling a spiritual need is believed to enjoy some divine sanction.

One pillar that seems to sustain this rather unorthodox theology is the African view of salvation. African Christians generally affirm the uniqueness of Jesus as the only savior of the world—but this affirmation stands in contradiction with their religious worldview, which is incurably pluralistic. Africans are generally hospitable to varied religious views. They are capable of participating in Islam, Christianity and African traditional rituals all in one day without fear of contradiction. The background to this thought is the African belief that God in his wisdom has a cause to let everything be; and

---

[15]http://www.africafiles.org/article.asp?ID=23410; retrieved on June 13, 2011.

that God could use different means or ways to heal, sustain, provide, prosper and even save. A casual conversation with most average Christian usually would reveal the implicit assumption that, different views of truth are seen as valid ways to God, and even when Christ is professed as *the way*, other ways are not necessarily disqualified. It is this pervasive belief that makes it difficult to uphold unadulterated loyalty to one faith alone, even when personal identity may be preferred to be associated with one faith and not many. The African concept of salvation is itself strongly tied with the concept of community, and hardly conceivable outside one's own community. Such ethnic loyalty, which secures good standing with the community, is believed to also automatically guarantee good standing with God.

In many ways, African Christianity is 'unchristian' even though it has huge Christian content. It can, pass for being 'Christian' because of its general outlook and presentation. African Christianity has smartly dressed itself in the Christian garb (history, terminologies, rituals, bible and sacraments). It is this garb which identifies African Christianity as Christian by concealing its true identity from the casual observer. After all, African communities do not have name for their 'religions' or a single founder of any of their belief systems as is the case with Buddhism, Confucianism or Christianity. Africans simply had religious traditions and that could as well be what today we are calling 'African Christianity,' that is, a religious way of life that identifies itself as 'Christianity' (rather uncritically) but is largely a 'Christianized' form of African traditional religion.

Lack of distinctive Christian ethics or doctrine, fledging loyalty and syncretistic tendencies make African Christianity largely superficial, ambiguous and inconsistent. African Christianity in this regard is like a bubble – lively, clear, huge, fun and attractive but characteristically fragile, lacking reflective grip and uncritically accommodative of all sorts of religious beliefs. It is possible that African Christianity will evolve a distinctive identity. We are beginning to see various emerging trends, which we shall explore in chapter four.

The current 'African Christianity' is part of the social fabric, the present cultural mould and rightfully claims a place among many threads that define African identity. Amidst the bubble and puff there is a sufficient critical mass of community of believers who will keep their candle burning and realize the hope for a stronger and more authentic African Christianity that will last well into the future but also stand the chance of inspiring a new social vision, with regard to the transformative power of the Gospel. The Gospel message needs to be applied in new ways that can shape new moral vision. Two things are essential in this regard: how the Church conducts mission on the one hand, and teaches Theology on the other. These two are our concerns in the next two chapters.

Conclusion

'African Christianity' forms only one thread among many that determine the identity of most 'African Christians.' Christianity has received impressive reception but still lives as a stranger within the African spiritual home. Many adherents accept and identify themselves with Christianity for reasons other than that of faith. As we have shown in this chapter, there are historical reasons that account for the current state of Christianity in Africa. Christianity's vision of new social reality, 'a new creation,' so to speak, demands that Christianity refuses to be simply part of the existing cultural mould. It needs to become the light that should guide the society. It should be the task of theology to seek effective ways of reintroducing Christianity in a new way. This can be done through critical theological education; formation of ecclesial grass root communities, emphases on biblical ethics and promotion of social tolerance and other such moral ideals.

Theology can also inform the church's mission. This is neither just about the 'translatability' of the Gospel nor planting denominational churches. It is about how Christianity can envision a better social ethic and alternate social realities. In this regard, the task of theology is to find ways of re-connecting the existing disconnects between beliefs and practices or between doctrines on the one hand, and ethics, morality and practice on the other. Christian values must find an interface with African values so as to help overcome the strange situation that currently prevails, where Christianity finds acceptance yet only as a garb over the traditional culture, and generally lacking the power to transform lives as it should.

Getting the mission of the church right is one way of addressing the existing disconnects. In the next chapter, we explore how this could be done.

CHAPTER TWO

Mission

Introduction

The question of 'how Christian is African Christianity,' rightly belongs to the subject matter of mission. A detour of sorts was necessary when we looked at this question in the previous chapter. We had to examine the historical background to African Christianity in order to determine why Africans accepted Christianity in large numbers, and to some extent the reasons for the shaky foundation of Christianity that was planted and perpetuated. We concluded that 'African Christianity' is for most part *unchristian*. In support for this claim, we apportioned the large part of blame to the way Western missionaries presented Christ to Africa and the context in which the evangelization of Africa took root. Christianity in Africa has failed to envision, influence and shape a better and alternative social vision for Africa because of its historical genesis and the context in which it was planted. Having faulted the western missionaries' approach to African mission, we propose in this chapter, that correct mission can help strengthen the shaky foundation of African Christianity. We suggest, by way of four proposed mission principles, ways of re-thinking mission if a more authentic and genuine Christianity can be established in Africa, and the seeming contradictions highlighted in chapter one can be addressed.

A Different Way of Doing Mission

How best can mission be carried out in Africa to support 'African Christianity' in concretizing the realization of the transformative power of the Gospel? Can mission be done differently so that the target of mission is not just about planting new churches but becomes more about the empowerment of believers in order to realize a better social reality in Africa, a reality built on just and equitable society? A caution would be helpful here. The title of this chapter may be seen as misleading. This is because we are not going to deal with a systematic exposition of the subject of mission in any conventional sense. We have rather chosen to briefly expound four themes that we have identified as the most basic biblical principles of mission. We must mention from the onset that biblical ideas of mission show that mission is an act of God as well as of the very nature of God. Our understanding of the nature of God necessarily informs our understanding of mission. Mission, for example, in the Christian sense is basically about a particular act, namely, the act of incarnation that reveals a God who in becoming a missioner becomes human and thereby enters into a special relationship with the entire human race. Mission in this sense is a revelatory historical event that continues to have historical significance. It is also at the same time, an attribute of God, that is, God is by nature a missioner God.

Besides being an attribute of God, Mission is also an act through which God connects with us and shapes or moulds our thoughts, our very being and spirituality. Mission as story of human liberation is definitely of the nature of God, his act as well as passion.[1] Consequently, being in God or in relationship with God means to participate in God's mission, and that to know God is to know God's mission. We also need to clarify from the onset that mission is relational as well as revelatory in the sense that the biblical God, whose nature is missional; achieves his missionary goals as an active relational and self-revealing God.

Mission is about God's sovereignty and willingness to make himself known and a story of how God renews history and reorients

---

[1] Cf. Christopher J. H. Wright, *The Mission of God: Unlocking the Bible's Grand Narrative,*" (IVP, USA, 2006), 44ff.

social reality. We shall proceed on the assumption that, the biblical God is unique and the only true God and that if the God of biblical revelation "is one true living God who made himself known in Israel and who wills to be known to the ends of the earth, then our mission can contemplate no lesser goal."[2] Mission begins with God who reaches his intended recipients through his chosen messengers like Noah, Abraham or Moses who in carrying out God's mandate must first seek to realign their will to the will of God.

Mission Begins with Self (Luke 4:23; Acts 1:8)

We cannot possibly exhaust all the biblical ideas of mission in such a short chapter or even a book. Some are more profound than others. Perhaps the profoundest mission principle of all is the mystery of the story of incarnation, where God not only entered into a special relationship with humanity but also did so in a rather radical way, by becoming human. Incarnation is God's model of mission and goes to the heart of God's mission to the world. Incarnation, the divine model of mission is built on love and grace of God and consequently begets a special relationship between God and humanity. One of the most loved and quoted verses of scripture best expresses this truth: 'For God so loved the world, that he gave his only begotten son that whomsoever believes in him, may not die but have everlasting life' (John 3:16). This verse underscores *one*—and only *one*—reason for God's mission to the world: *love*—a love that compels God to descend to the level of his creatures in becoming one with them. It is for this purpose that, 'the word became flesh and dwelt among us' (John 1:14) or as the Nicene Creed affirms; 'he became man for us and for our salvation.'

Going by this, God's mission method could be understood as incarnational. The model is best expressed in Jesus' fulfillment of the mission of God to the world. We learn one cardinal truth from

---

[2]Christopher J. H. Wright, *The Mission of God: Unlocking the Bible's Grand Narrative*," (IVP, USA, 2006), 71.

this method – that mission is inseparable from the missioner. God did not only reach out in mission but also incarnated himself to carry out his mission. In the mission of God, the act and being of God are inseparable. Far from patronage, God's approach is that of self-abasement in reaching the other, thereby creating a relationship of mutuality and service.

The apostle Paul beautifully summarizes the incarnational model of mission in the following words which are recorded in his letter to the Philippians 2:6-8: 'Christ Jesus, though in the form of God, did not count equality with God a thing to be grasped, but emptied himself, taking the form of a servant ... and being found in human form he humbled himself and became obedient unto death, even death on the cross.' The incarnational model is kenotic. *Kenosis* is the Greek word from which we get the English translation, 'emptied himself.' It basically means that Christ limited, renounced, or put aside his divine attributes in order to identify himself with humanity. It is a total giving of self for the purpose of accomplishing the intended mission—and this at no mean price including self renunciation and even death.

For this to be possible, Christ had to bring his will in total conformity with the will of God. This was never easy even for Jesus, who though fully God was also equally human. The story of Gethsemane is perhaps the best example of the ultimate battle of wills. 'Should I carry out God's mission regardless ... or should I count the cost and take the easier option at the risk of failure to carry out the intended mission?' Jesus' conclusion is arguably one of the most difficult prayers anyone could have ever offered, and the toughest battle of wills, for that matter, a prayer we all would rather avoid: 'Father, your will be done, not mine' (Luke.22:42)

But 'your will be done' is the missioner's prayer; and the missioner can never effectively carry out the mission of God unless he or she has first totally submitted to the will of God who sends. This involves, among other things, a 'mission to self' – which we propose as the first principle of mission: that, unless you first minister to yourself with conviction, you can never effectively minister to anyone. To succeed in this we need to have the mind of Jesus, which was characterized by single focus and a purpose to rise above self-interest in pursuance of the interests of the one who sent him. It takes us back to what we said in the beginning: mission is relational and revelatory. It is about seeking clarity about 'the will of God' and at the same time getting our relationship with God right. The paradox with this model is that you do not seek personal growth or glory, even though with the growth and glorification of God and God's work, the obedient missioner eventually will realize growth and glory. The incarnational model also envisions—that we meaningfully become one with those to whom we are sent. The mission of God in this sense is always a mission from within. It takes a cultural residence thereby giving the Incarnate One a cultural expression through which the revelation of God is communicated in understandable cultural codes. Christ the God Incarnate assumed a host culture and revealed God from within that host culture. Similarly the Gospel in Africa must incarnate within the Africa host culture; and thereby be communicated in the African tone and accent. This is absolutely necessary if the gospel of life is to be understood and its relevance and liberating power realized.

African Christianity has a strange dual nature. Although Christianity largely has been accepted, the power of the Gospel is yet to be fully appreciated as the primary reference point for moral, ethical or even religious orientation and judgment. Although Christianity is domiciled in Africa, it has yet remained a stranger within the African cultural and religious milieu. As discussed in Chapter One above, even though Christianity has been embraced by African masses yet it remains a stranger of sorts because we have neither fully 'owned' nor appropriately appropriated as our spiritual home. Faith-claims and practices are often remain disconnected revealing a glaring dichotomy or contradictions of sorts. For Christianity to be fully rooted and understood there is need to inculturate the gospel message by re-expressing, reinterpreting and reapplying the gospel truth using the right cultural codes, meaningful thought forms and relevant images. The incarnational model of mission inspires inculturation and in following the example of Christ, makes the cultural rebirth of the gospel message imperative for mission.

This means that our first mission, based on biblical perspective of incarnation should be to the church itself. Let the evangelization of the world begin with the re-evangelization of the church. It is only when we have secured Jerusalem that we can confidently move out to Samaria and to the ends of the world (Acts.1:8 cf. Luke 4:23). Just as is the case with individual believer where mission must begin with self, the African church must first put its house in order by clarifying its mission mandate, and renewing its vision for effective engagement with the world.

One historical baggage of the African church is the dichotomy between the preacher and the recipient of the Word; epitomized in the colonizer and the colonized images of social reality. The result of such non-incarnational approach can cause resentment or may even breed contemptuous attitude as, 'physician first heal yourself.' It is a paradox that even though the Word of God found a fertile ground in the African heart, yet ironically the ground was smothered and hardened under the heavy trod of the sower himself!

Mission is *missio Dei*, not *missio homo* (Matt.28:19; John 20:21; John 17:18)

The Bible as a whole is contextualized by references to God who continuously reaches out to his creation. The whole of the bible is contextualized by God's missional involvement with the world. Indeed the bible is one big story of mission; and that God's mission must form the basis of the church's mission activities. This brings me to the second biblical principle: that of 'mission as *missio Dei*, not *missio homo*.' This also brings to our attention a basic theological truth that mission is not just a function of God, but an essential attribute of God's nature. God cannot be but a Missionary God because mission is not just an *act* (like an isolated incident) but of the nature of God's very being. Simply put, mission is an attribute of a Missionary God who is actively involved with his world. This has significant implications for our understanding of mission. To be a missioner, for example, one has to be in relationship with God, that is, God who is the missioner and who yet is also the principal subject and the real meaning of mission. It also means that mission is of God or *missio Dei*. The Latin phrase *Missio Dei*, means 'the sending of God,' underscoring that mission primarily is not about '*missio homo*;' 'the sending of man.' It is only by entering and staying in relationship with God that we become active participants in the being of God and the activity of God, namely, God's mission.

While mission has the nature of sending, correctly applied to man, *missio Dei* is not the sending of man by God, but rather an invitation from God to humanity to participate in *the* mission, which is always the mission of God. The invitation is to the church, a redeemed humanity that is called out and constituted in the first place as a result of God's missionary activity in the world. This makes it clear why mission does not exist because of the church, but the church exists because of mission. Put another way, there is church because there is mission, and not the other way round. It is, therefore, imperative for the Church to get her mission right if an authentic and strong Christianity capable of empowering and transforming lives is to be realized.

African Christianity today is largely ineffective because we have lost this fundamental difference. Thanks to our historical origins, we have made *missio Dei,* into *missio homo*. We have assumed that the mission to the world is the mission of the church to which we can invite God to go with us. We have turned a basic biblical principle upside down forgetting that it is not us inviting God to mission work but that it is God who is inviting us to his mission to the world; we have assumed we are sent to carry out God's mission when in fact we are only asked to participate. Our mission mandate should clearly be based on our being in relationship with God – the beginning point from which all other things must follow. As invited participants, believers are tasked to provide the medium through which God's redemptive activity can touch the world. Like Jesus, the incarnate-

God, believers are called to be 'God-bearers' (*theotokos*) in clarifying, fulfilling and furthering God's mission in the world.

The church has turned *missio Dei* into *missio homo*—building denominational empires in the name of the Kingdom of God. Our sorry state reminds me of my church's liturgy of confession – which comes closer to anything that I know in helpfully describing the situation in which we live as a church. We usually confess and say: 'we have done wrong and neglected to do right; we have done what we ought not to have done and have not done what we ought to have done...' this liturgical formula of confession is about personal state of sinfulness and not as such about mission. But the wording of this prayer helpfully serves well to express our twisted view of mission. Our misconception about the true meaning of *missio Dei*, has often led us to push our agenda in the name of God's agenda. We have labored to fulfill our earthly goals in the name of fulfilling God's mission. As a result we have ended up having, too much of the world in the church and too little of the church in the world. There are a number of reasons for this prevailing state of affairs. One example of such reasons will suffice to help make the point.

Scientific and cultural progresses, as well as intellectual and technological advancements have increasingly continued to nurture seeds of doubt regarding the truth of faith-claims and value of religious practices. As a result, large populations of educated folk regard religion merely as a relic of a dying culture or at best a matter of personal or private affair. The African church, desperate to stay relevant and pushed by these trends is increasingly secularizing. Clear patterns of world-church relationship are emerging where the world sets the pace and the agenda, and the Church plays the catch up game. It is true that in almost any sphere of life—the environment; poverty; social- cultural trends; politics and governance; business, commerce or economics, and entertainment—the church takes the cue from the world. Mission is beginning to be understood as the adaptation of that which would make the Church as close to the world as may be possible; and that the motto of such mission is: 'what the world can do, the church can do better.' A good example is in worship and liturgical innovations where grammar, concepts, presentation and application of secular forms of art and music often are uncritically adopted for most modern services.

We clarify that there is no intention at all here to disparage the importance of the transmission of biblical message that definitely contributes to complex learning as well as social and cultural personal effectiveness which go beyond the primary purpose of mission itself.[3] In principle there may be nothing wrong with such trends, but there is always the danger of confusing what is acceptable, with what is right. Given that what is acceptable is not necessarily what is right; any uncritical or inappropriate mission strategy or principle can run the risk of compromise, loosing direction or appropriate sense of judgment and even the truth. When the Church blindly follows every worldly trend in the name of staying relevant, there is always the danger of darkness overcoming the light. The consequence of one blind leading another is anyone's guess. The ineffectiveness of Christianity is due to its failure to tell a distinctively different story, to shape different identities, envision new social realities and break the problematic African cultural mould.

It is because of the church's misconception of the mission of God in that many would today identify themselves as Christians and yet can find it easy to "take leave of God without taking leave of the church."[4] This explains why numerous 'followers' will value church membership if only to belong somewhere but without any serious commitment towards the teachings of the Church or the Gospel imperative regarding moral responsibility or social communion. It also explains why a country said to be over '95% Christian' can easily dispense with the two dimensional law of love of God and neighbor and can carry out ethnic cleansing of fellow Christians, or, that a country rated as '80% Christian' also tops the list of most

---

[3]Michael Sievernich, *Christian Mission*, (Mainz: Institute of European History, 2011), 45.
[4]Gerald Bray, *Creeds, Councils and Christ,* (Leceister, IVP, 1984), 7.

corrupt countries in the world. These and such other trends are indicative of a mission terribly gone wrong where *missio homo* has created *a Christianity* with no Christ at the centre; with no ethical and moral reference to write home about.

The Church in Africa has embraced numbers and outward form of religion without transformation – resulting into a schizophrenic religiosity where doctrine is not always translated into practical matters of ethics. As Gerald Bray observes,

> The so-called 'progressive churches' "cannot escape from the charge that they have replaced [theological depth] with religious entertainment, and that the doctrinal backbone to their preaching is decidedly weak. Many have no idea that creeds and confessions are an essential aid to Christian growth, and that the quality of our spiritual life is directly dependent on our understanding of theological truth.[5]

Bible waving and noisy display of spirituality with promises of health and prosperity has become the outward marks of the assurance of salvation. The church has become too comfortable in earthly pursuits that the Offence of the Cross (I Cor.1:18) has increasingly become a strange Gospel to a majority of African Christians.

Driven by the desire to command mass followings, build financial base, amass power, and secure recognition, churches often fall for 'what the world wants to hear' and in the process have lost the sense of 'what the world should hear.' No wonder our churches are filled with enthusiastic worshippers who flock the churches for what has come to be called 'spiritual makeover' or 'power-sessions' and 'inspirational doses'. The worshippers typically would move 'heaven and earth,' so to speak, in their praise and worship although at the same time they can lie and cheat, steal and commit adultery without a second thought or reference to the faith they claim to profess. It is very possible that this sad state of affairs is as a result

---

[5]Ibid., 8.

of our failure to understand, accept and apply the biblical principles of mission as *missio Dei*. African Christianity is guilty of conforming too much to the patterns of the secular culture and social realities, thereby reducing Mission of God into a mission to satisfy human culture. The correct understanding of mission, as *missio Dei*, can correct our defective mission practices and inform our strategies.

Christianity as We Know it Must Die, that Faith May Live
(John 12:24 cf. Mark 10:45; Gal.2:20)

The third biblical principle of mission that I am proposing is a principle that takes at its centre the model of the Cross. The Cross is one of the profoundest mysteries of God's ways with the world. Jesus came so as to die. What a mission! We are wrong if we think he came to establish a religion of sorts, or even a super-religion for that matter. He was not born into a religion-less world, but a world highly religious in many different ways. He showed a way of which religion was not the essence of spiritual wellbeing but only the outward form of spirituality or a vehicle for spiritual expression. Like the Pharisees of old whom Jesus accused of hypocritically paying tithes on herbs, and too concerned with right conduct of rituals at the expense of the higher demands of love and mercy. The Church too today specializes in religion at the expense of the weightier matters of the Gospel. How else can we explain African Christianity's inadequacy in providing a workable social model as an alternative to such destructive dominant models, as for example, negative ethnicity?

The African Church has concentrated too much on the outward form – committees, boards, tithes, buildings, numbers, networks, rituals, ceremonies, entertainments, Sunday services, week day fellowships, Christmas and Easter festivities. These forms are essential but are not integral or core to Christian faith. The outward form of religion is neither mission nor is it necessarily liberating. The outward forms of religion do not necessarily belong to the very essence of mission. Indeed, the forms often have become modern types of idolatry. Even though faith that transforms must necessarily shape and inform the outward forms, the correctness of the form must never be mistaken for the correctness of faith. A church that just simply 'thrives' on structures and forms soon becomes just one more thread in the fabric of the cultural mould and fails to create desired social ethic and an alternative social reality.

We often are deluded in thinking that the outward form of things is one and the same with the inner reality of things. For our context—the signs are already in place—we have people who are very religious—and zealously display religiosity and perpetuate their beliefs in all forms of ways yet they have lost the essence of the very faith they profess—such that there is a great chasm between faith and practice with a disturbing disconnect especially between doctrine and ethics. To pray with the Lord's Prayer or recite the creed has become a simple liturgical 'exercise', and hollow spiritual claims, is never a problem for most worshippers. It is not far from truth to claim, for example, that at anyone time half of any congregation will happily join in with others to say – unashamedly and loudly, *'forgive us our sins as we forgive those who sin against us'* and without meaning it at all, or without any intention, whatsoever, to act on what they say. Herein the Church fails to grasp the power that otherwise comes with the creation of a 'forgiving and forgiven community.'

The Biblical principle of mission that uses the model of the Cross challenges the hollow spirituality of 'uncritical' Christianity. The Cross is a symbol of brokenness, forgiveness and reconciliation but also a symbol of judgment – calling the self-righteous to die to self so as to live to Christ. Seen in the light of the cross, Christianity that has continued to survive on 'outward religious forms' and mere display of self-righteous spirituality must die. As Christ died to give life, so must Christianity of convenience, egoistic spirit and empty traditions die to give a chance to a living faith – a faith not dependent for survival on numbers, conformity to cultural trends, financial power or entertainments but the sacrificial model of the power of the Cross. Mission must correct the unashamed, self-righteous

Christianity of "whitewashed tombs, which outwardly appear beautiful but inside is filled with deadness and decay" (Matt.23:27). The African church must ask: why is there such impressive enthusiasm and vibrant numerical growth yet such disconnects between what followers say they believe and how their moral and ethical living is ordered?

Mission is about correct teaching and praxis. The two are inextricably intertwined because orthodoxy informs orthopraxis. For example, how can one confess the belief in a God of justice and at the same time participate in a corrupt and unjust system? Right teaching (orthodoxy) and right practice (orthopraxis), both demand that the road to life is via death such that, 'unless the grain of wheat falls to the ground and dies, it remains alone; but if it dies, it bears much fruit' (John 12:24 cf. Mark 10:45). This means the values of the world are often in conflict with those of the Kingdom. To be first, for example, one must accept to be last, and that blessed are the poor, lowly, oppressed or persecuted. This is a strange teaching to modern ears and hard to accept. In the practical sense it means that Christianity of cheap grace, easy options and convenience must die, for mission to succeed and for a living faith to flourish. On a practical level, the church needs to re-learn Christianity by extricating it from the cultural mould that has reduced African Christianity to just one other thread in the envisioning and creation of our social reality and identities.

The outward visible form of a successful mission is manifest in transformed lives; and for the new transformed life to take root, the old must be uprooted in the pattern of Jeremiah's mission (Jer.1:10). Or as Paul puts it, the old nature must die that the believer may rise as a new creation (2 Cor.5:17). Mission is biblical and effective only when following the ways of God one yields to the cultivation of individual moral responsibility and social communion (*koinonia*), and consequently makes possible the abundance of life for which God became incarnate (John 10:10; Luke 4:18). This calls for a new kind of social engagement that must be informed by the basic gospel reality of incarnation, which ironically invites the believer to die in order to live.

Mission is Not About Power, but About Charisma
(cf. Isa.1:18; Matt.21:5; John 1:11-12)

Our fourth and last proposal is that unlike what seems to be a common understanding of mission in Africa, mission is not about simply 'church planting' and the power that comes with numerical growth, but about charisma. Unfortunately, our understanding of the nature of God is often influenced not so much by God's own revelation, but rather by ascribing to God what we often would like to ascribe to ourselves. As Ludwig Feuerbach argued a century ago, we tend to objectify our deepest desires and make them into a god whom we create in our own image, an image that often lacks meaning and clarity other than those that we accord it. A good example is the attribute of God's power or his omnipotence. Absolute power is an attribute of God that God chooses not to actualize in the absolute sense but only keeps it as potential or tentative. What this means is that God needs not use his power to achieve his goal; he uses personal appeal or charisma to win his creation over to his point of view. As Rev.3:20 say, God does not force his way into any heart but knocks and waits for invitation from the willing heart.

The Cross is the perfect example here. God at a moment of powerlessness and vulnerability died at the hands of his creatures. He did not rain fire from heaven but willingly went down to hell; he did not struck his attackers blind; but accepted to be blind-folded and robbed of his sight. He did not display his might and power but allowed his distracters to render him powerless. In deed, even when he victoriously overcame death he quietly and discreetly ascended into the clouds; and did not show himself or prove anything to those who rejected and killed him. He simply accomplished his mission – not by power, but love. His principle was simply; 'he who has ears let him hear, he who has eyes let him see, and let the willing heart accept.'

This principle goes to the heart of the Gospel. On one occasion when Jesus realized that his disciples were so obsessed by earthly powers and knowing that they cannot be trusted to put the needs of others and the will of God before their own desire for power, he told them: 'whoever wants to be first, must be last of all and servant of all' (Mark 9:35). Using the child as an example of innocence and powerlessness, Jesus clarifies that the way to salvation (itself a matrix of power and the goal of mission) is found in embracing powerlessness for the purpose of service. No wonder the message of the gospel is foolishness to the world; but the foolishness of God is wiser than all human wisdom (1 Cor. 1:25). It may not make sense, but the right route to gaining power is through powerlessness, where in giving one receives, and in dying one lives.

Power may be defined in different ways. In the New Testament, power is closely associated with God's grace as in, for example, the power that saves or heals. I would like to differentiate the New Testament understanding of power (Greek – *dunamis*) from a more commonplace understanding of power today. Correctly interpreted, the New Testament *dunamis* refers to the dynamic force of the Holy Spirit working in and through a believer for the purpose of healing the sick, delivering the oppressed, preaching the Gospel and victorious spiritual living in the power of the Spirit. Power, as understood by most people in the Kenyan context today is a coping mechanism for sustained control or influence over others. In its most raw form; it has four basic elements: manipulation; desire; coercion or force and fear of losing power. To actualize or exercise power means to live on the edge or commit oneself to any one or all of these elements. It will be worthwhile to clarify briefly each of these elements.

Manipulation is about predetermining results and using whatever means to win others over to your point of view. It acts on implicit threats to others and their vulnerability and seeks to preempt any opposition. The root cause of manipulation is desire.

Desire is about attachment, which in itself is not a bad thing. When power is misapplied desire for power becomes addictive. We often hear of the phrase; 'power is like an intoxicating drink, it becomes very difficult to shake it off once it gets into our heads.' The desire to have more power and to stay in power for as long as possible is always stronger than the desire to let go. Power that is driven by addictive desire becomes obsessive and never liberating. It will do anything, including coercion or use of force to have its way.

Coercion is an extreme form of manipulation. Power has always the potential for violence; and when people who are in power are drunk or are 'high' on power, they tend to loose direction; and often resort to coercion or outright force so as to have their way. The bottom-line of what drives them is actually fear, and especially the fear of losing power.

Fear is an important ingredient of a well balanced emotional state of being. On the positive extreme, fear is associated with wisdom, as in, for example, fear of God being the beginning of all wisdom, yet on the negative extreme fear also borders on irrationality. People in power are often on the negative end of this spectrum. They generally are suspicious and fearful. Their biggest fear is the 'loss of power' where the most haunting thought is often: what will happen to me if or when I am no longer in charge? They assume invincibility and seek immortality, and in the process often lose touch with reality.

The biblical principle of mission is not about this kind of power but basically about charisma. The word charisma simply means gift, giftedness or more specifically divine favor. It is the art of envisioning an inclusive humanity, and the translation of every potentiality into the actualization of the fullness of life, which is the primary goal of God's mission to the world. To do this, Christianity must re-engineer a different social ethic, a new way of seeing and understanding the world and a new way of belonging.

The Church today seems to have lost this basic mission principle. We witness a leadership that has built personal empires in the name of the Kingdom of God. We witness a leadership that being drunk with power has dethroned Christ and enthroned itself. Church leadership has become a means to an end, an opportunity to establish selfish personal ambitions that would stop at nothing in the quest to fulfill this desire. We need to return to the biblical basics that leadership is not about power but about charisma. It is not about loarding it over others but service, not self seeking but giving. The shallowness of African Christianity is really due to failure to appreciate this true meaning of mission.

Conclusion: Re-thinking Mission

In this chapter, we deliberately avoided looking at mission in the more usual way that the subject is commonly expounded. We have chosen not to deal with textual exegesis or carry out any close examination of God's ways of dealing with humanity in the history of salvation; or discuss mission mandate, for that matter. The list of principles discussed here are not at all exhaustive but meant to provide us with a framework to outline at least four basic principles that go to the very heart of the biblical nature of mission. Our basic conviction is that an effective mission is a mission that necessarily begins with God. On this basis, the missioner cannot effectively minister to anyone unless is first convinced of the power of the Gospel and willing to accept God's ways with the world, that is, the Incarnation (birth) and the Cross (death). In the practical sense, the Church needs to adopt God's way of mission for effective service to God and God's world if the desired goal of transformation and the abundance of life that the Bible talks about is to be realized.

The churches in Africa today are often captive to power struggles and leadership wrangles. Territorial expansions, quantitative growth, financial returns and partisan politics often undermine effective mission that would otherwise truly enhance the Kingdom of God that can bring about real social change and contribute to the creation of a just society. There is need to think mission as *missio Dei*, putting Christ at the centre of it all. Re-orienting our mission focus towards God and God's will for the world, will afford us the possibility to correct the commonplace misconception, which usually measures mission success or institutional accomplishments by the yardstick of financial base, power or positions, status and numerical strength. It will also afford us the fruit of the true Gospel, the power that can break the circle of violence, oppression, divisive politics, corruption and exploitation that currently African Christianity has failed to address or provide alternative models of social reality.

The authenticity and genuineness of African Christianity must be measured against visible fruitfulness in terms of transformed lives and changed moral and ethical orientations that can entrench justice and eradicate oppressive social-economic and political structures. This is possible only if God is at the centre of all that we do in discharge of mission. The word of God demands our all – including death—to self—in submitting our will in totality to God's will. The visible result that is expected should be enhanced individual responsibility and social communion. Only then can we tell whether the Church is truly a missioner participant or merely exploiting the name of God as a business associate for help in accomplishing its own mission. To get its mission right, the Church needs the right theology possible through a sound program of theological education. This latter is our concern in the next chapter.

CHAPTER THREE

Theological Education

Introduction

In a paper published in the 90s, C.B. Peter observes that "There is need to wean Christian Theology away from the Western breast and feed it on African porridge."[1] This observation stands as true as when it was first written. Ironically, African Christianity today is growing faster than that of the West but on the theological diet of Western Christianity. Could this account for the fact that African Christianity's numerical strength is not matched by its theological depth? How comes that Christianity in Africa is one of the fastest growing, yet suffers such a puzzling superficiality and disconnects, which we outlined in chapter one above? In this chapter, we propose that lack of relevant and adequate theological education could account for such paradoxes. We contend that right theological education is the key to the realization of a strong Christianity that can be effective in bringing about the transformative power of the Gospel.

African Christianity: Phenomenal Numerical Strength
Philip Jenkins in his book, *The Next Christendom: The Coming of Global Christianity* writes:

---

[1] C. B. Peter, "African Hyphenated Christians – an Alternate Model of Theologizing in Africa," in Nordic Journal of African Studies 3(1), 1994, 103.

We are currently living through one of the transforming moments in the history of religion worldwide. Over the past five centuries or so, the story of Christianity has been inextricably bound up with that of Europe and European derived civilizations overseas, above all in North America. Until recently the overwhelming majority of Christians have lived in White nations, allowing theorists to speak smugly, arrogantly, of "European Christian" civilization. Conversely, radical writers have seen Christianity as the religion of the "West" or, to use another popular metaphor, the global North.[2]

It appears that Christianity is finding 'new homes' in places where Christianity has traditionally been a minority religion. As Jenkins again observes, "Over the past century ... the centre of gravity in the Christian world has shifted inexorably southward, to Africa, Asia, and Latin America."[3] Although Jenkins' observation is spot on, the theologies and Christianity of these new churches (The Global South) are in themselves a perpetuation of 'Western' Christianity. There is an increasing sense of disillusionment with the use of 'Western' models in the teaching of theology in Africa. Most of the new churches are struggling to find their true identity and grounding when it comes to a theology that can nurture and sustain an authentic and truly indigenous Christianity. The quest for an indigenous Christianity, identity and relevant theology has been hampered by a variety of factors, and not least due to an overbearing western cultural domination and perpetual mentorship.

To ascertain the strength of 'emerging' Christianity one may need to critically examine history of Christianity, its present trends, demographic distribution of Christian communities, the effectiveness with regard to the power of the Gospel in transforming societies, and more importantly, the quality and strength of contextualization to guide the interpretation and appropriation of beliefs. It is important to acknowledge that numbers may in themselves, not necessarily be the sufficient yardstick to measure the strength, mission, relevance

---
[2] 2002, 1-2.
[3] ibid, 2.

and the theological depth of any church. The churches of the two-thirds world are definitely registering phenomenal success in terms of numbers. In some of these places churches are registering the fastest growth rates ever recorded in the history of Christianity. The existing records and projections are really remarkable. According to *World Christian Encyclopedia*:

> Some 2 billion Christians are alive today, about one-third of the planetary total. The largest single bloc, some 560 million people, is still to be found in Europe. Latin America, though, is already close behind with 480 million. Africa has 360 million, and 313 million Asians profess Christianity. North America claims about 260 million believers.[4]

Jenkins, who makes a detailed study of these figures, also makes this helpful projection:

> If we extrapolate these figures to 2025, and assume no great gains or losses through conversion, then there would be around 2.6 billion Christians, of whom 633 million would live in Africa, 640 million in Latin America, and 460 million in Asia. Europe with 555 million, would have slipped to third place.[5]

It is worth noting that two of the third world continents, Africa and Latin America will be neck to neck competing for the leading place as the continent with most Christians on earth. The rate of church growth in these two places is simply extraordinary in comparison to the trends in other parts of the world. In Africa alone, "the number of Christians increased, staggeringly, from 10 million in 1900 to 360 million by 2000."[6] If numbers are anything to go by, these figures are a sure indication that "there can be no doubt that the emerging

---

[4] ibid, 2-3.
[5] ibid, 3.
[6] ibid, 4.

Christian world will be anchored in the Southern continents."[7] It must be noted that, demography is not the only indicator, and perhaps should be the least preferred indicator for determining the spiritual health or theological depth and soundness of a church. Also, the world is becoming increasing a complex entity where distinctions based on demography, religion or even culture are no longer as clear as it has always been.

A Good Theological Education is Needed for A Good Theology
Seen in light of the current global realities, especially the fact of globalization, advancements in communication, and the unprecedented levels of immigration of individuals or whole peoples from one part of the world to another, any neat categorization of theology is bound to fail. Also, although the Church's numerical strength is very important, it is, however, more important to ascertain the relevancy of the Church by the way the Church's teachings and mission can influence and transform society. This will help us determine whether Christianity in Africa will continue to flourish and be seen to be truly 'the salt of the earth' and 'the light of the world.' This is the calling of any church, and if the church has to be effective a contextually appropriate, relevant and workable program of theological education is imperative. Here, we deliberately emphasis theological education. This is because a strong church is not built simply on numbers but on the strength of its faith, for which theological education is imperative.

There are numerous challenges to achieving relevant and quality theological education in Africa today. To mention a few of these challenges: theological education is faced by lack of adequate resources and suffers captivity to Western theology. These key challenges are further compounded by a context of religious and cultural pluralism and a shallow spirituality or superficiality, globalization and increasing socio-cultural changes that seem to go hand in hand with secularization of religious communities. In Africa,

---
[7] ibid, 14.

these challenges are further complicated by difficult situations that face the communities of faith including persistent wars, poor governance, endemic corruptions, HIV and AIDS prevalence, the poverty and suffering that goes with it, as well as, exploitation or injustices often perpetrated on one another by people who claim to share the same values and profess the same faith. This is not only a source of ridicule for African Christianity, but also serves to portray African Christianity as a mere outward religiosity that lacks moral value or theological integrity and depth.

Perceptive scholars have, however, had reason to believe in the emergence of a credible "Third Church," to use a phrase first coined by Walbert Buhlmann on the analogy of the 'third world.' Andrew Walls, the respected History of Missions scholar also has no doubt of the credibility of the 'Third Church' or of its theology. Walls is confident that, "Faith in Africa is a distinctive new tradition of Christianity comparable to Catholicism, Protestantism, [and] Orthodoxy." He further asserts, "It is the standard Christianity of the present age, a demonstration model of its character."[8] While these writers cannot be accused for simply pegging their judgments on numerical strength alone, their assessment are, however, understandably sympathetic.

One rather disturbing phenomenon is the existence of serious tensions at the very core of this celebrated 'standard Christianity.' The existing tensions do not only present formidable challenges but also cast doubt on the very integrity of Christianity in Africa. These tensions have direct bearing on theological education and training, and need to be addressed as direct challenges to theology. There is, for example, a disturbing disconnect between African theology and spirituality; and an equally disturbing disconnect between doctrine and ethics; all of which are, at the end of the day, a reflection of an existing chasm, by and large, between faith and practice. It would be reasonable to suggest that African Christianity can only become "the standard Christianity" if the quantitative growth of the church

---

[8]ibid, 4.

in Africa is matched by qualitative growth that is supported and shaped by a credible and relevant program of theological education.

What is desperately needed is a theology that is able to address the numerous disconnects now typical of African Christianity, a theology that is able to shape the emergence of a Christianity that is as orthodox as it is indigenous. It is possible that the existing disconnects are as a result of Africa's continued use of western models of theological education, and alien cultural and theological categories, which perhaps are, for most part, ill suited for the African context.

Models of Theological Education in Africa

Africans have continued, for all sorts of reasons, to indulge in Western theological education. They are trained in and work with Western philosophical and theological categories, Western hermeneutical and exegetical methods, and generally grapple with questions that basically arise from the Western historical and present contextual realities and perspectives. Although most African theological educators largely work with such inherited theological models that are often alien to their African context, most also work hard to abandon or discard the Western models within which their theological reflections and training were shaped. As Musa Dube observes, for example:

> Almost all, if not all, Black African scholars of the last twenty years were trained in Western schools ... steeped in the historical critical methods of biblical studies, yet the assessment of their works indicates that most of them took a different approach from their training.[9]

Dube makes an interesting observation that most African theological scholars although trained in the West and are well versed with the

---

[9]"Current Issues in Biblical Interpretation," in *Theological Education in Contemporary Africa*, LeMarquand & Galgalo (eds.) (Eldoret, Zapf Chancery, 2004), 39-61, 53.

western approaches to theology, yet have chosen to map a totally different path for how theology could best be done in Africa. This is an indication that the western methodological frameworks that they learned are either irrelevant or inadequate for the African context. Consequently, African theologians have chosen to grapple with models that can hopefully 'incarnate Christ in Africa' in a way that the Christian faith can become more meaningful and practical.

According to John Parratt, three factors seem to emerge as the fundamental determinants for the methodological framework: "the Bible and Christian tradition, African culture and religion, and social-political situation."[10] These three basic factors have continued to influence theological interpretations that emphasize one or another kind of socio-political, cultural or spiritual needs as context or situation may demand. These efforts have given rise to distinctive types of African theologies or 'African theological models' such as adaptation, localization, indigenization, inculturation, contextualization, liberation, and reconstruction. Whereas the efforts of African theologians to 'incarnate Christ in Africa' by way of these methods are commendable, there is a worrying trend that their impact on the church at the grassroots is minimal.

Perhaps the best example I could give is that of African 'inculturation' Christology. This is a subject that is most debated and written about by African theologians. One interesting interpretation, that employs the inculturation method, is how trained theologians employ conceptual categories from African cultures to construct a Christology purportedly relevant to the African context. These categories although rightly inspired by African cultural milieu and world view, but are formulated in the academies, published for the consumption of the academies, and remain within the academies. I am yet to hear, for example, a sermon from a church pulpit that presents Christ as an African ancestor. The academy does its own thing and so does the church, and this raises serious questions about

---

[10]John Parratt, *Reinventing Christianity* (Grand Rapids: Eerdmans, 1995), 2.

theological substance and value when it comes to either a church that does not take theological reflection of its faith seriously, or an academy whose theological signposts are mainly for building of personal curriculum vitae, scholarly expediency and most of the time, simply incomprehensible to the ordinary Church-goers. "In such circumstances," observes Gerald Bray, "it is hardly surprising that the person in the pew is often scandalized by academic theology, and prefers to regard it as irrelevant, or even hostile to professed beliefs."[11]

It is the task of theological education to take this as a serious challenge and formulate theologies and theological models that are relevant and practically useful for the church's consumption. With regard to such task, I have an idea of how we may proceed.

To start with, the western theological models that were received are varied and none are inherently impotent or useless for the African context, but a lot depends on how these models are appropriated for a specific African cultural and religious situation. There is need for evaluating each model for their effectiveness before they either are considered for application or set aside wholesale.

Structural Models

What we inherited from the West is not one model but a number of models. According to the most common analysis, "There have been three basic models that have shaped the history of theological education."[12] The three are commonly identified as: classical model, German graduate school model and the third, especially associated with Charles Fielding[13] is the professional model. In my view, these models are of three types. They are models of structure, models of curriculum and models of hermeneutics. We shall use these three

---

[11]Gerald Bray, *Creeds, Councils and Christ* (Leceister, IVP, 1984), 8.
[12]http://goliath.ecnext.com/coms2/gi_0199-4190911/Where-do-ministers-come-from.html.
[13]ibid.

types for the purpose of our analysis; and regard these others – classical, graduate school and professional as the sub-set of my three broad types.

The *classical model* is a model where a theological institution prepared students for ordained ministry for a specific denomination. The classical model typically adapts a residential school system where ordinands live and learn together as a community for a specified period of time. The students follow a strict regime of spiritual formation, where personal devotion and clarity of vocation is emphasized. The classroom and by extension the library and chapel are the contexts of learning. The classical model is a 'structural type' model where theological education is rigidly placed within the context of formal structures – structured curriculum, structured schedules or timeframe (prescribed years of study) and structured space of learning.

One major weakness of the classical model as applied in the African context is that a totally institution-based training cannot prepare students to adequately face the challenges presented by contemporary pastoral settings. The three or four years of residential training may be suited to prepare scholars and sharpen skills of library based research but is not quite suited for service out of the academy. I propose that the wider world, and not just the theological community or institution, should be the primary context of training. That way, theological training will be more focused on theological issues generated by reflective practice and becomes a life-long learning exercise. This model where learning takes place in the wider pastoral context, and the curriculum is shaped by theological questions arising from the context, and where theological education is ideally life-long rather than timed, can be called 'the project model.'

The *project model* of learning should be informed by two major sources. These are the classical sources (including the bible and Christian traditions) and experiential sources (including on-going research, reflective practice, real life experiences and dynamics of faith expressions within the communities of faith). The project model is characteristically cyclic in the way it operates. At the heart of it is a reflective practice that keeps revisiting earlier questions, premises, research findings, conclusions and then beginning over again in light of new insights. Just as a caveat, St. Paul's University in Limuru, Kenya, provides an excellent example of such model of study with regard to some of its ground breaking initiatives in initiating reflective, practical and community based theological programs in specific areas of study like HIV and AIDS, and Development Studies.

The *German graduate school model* resulted when theological colleges translated into universities or became affiliated to a university. The emphasis in the graduate school model shifted from spiritual and ministerial formation to intellectual pursuits. Theology was considered to be an academic discipline like any other and that its scholarship must be as credible as any other discipline such as law, architecture, engineering and medicine. While the model still accommodates the training of ministers, it nevertheless transcends denominational and confessional specificity and embraces the university spirit of openness. With all its shortcomings, especially regarding the nature and quality of theological, ministerial and spiritual formation; the model is currently gaining popularity in Africa where most theological colleges are either busy translating themselves into universities or seeking affiliation with a university to accredit their theological programs. As Brian Hill observes:

> Most theological seminaries for status reasons covet comparison with universities ... seeking accreditation within the academic community at the cost of innovations they would like to introduce, because literary-academic criteria tend, in universities, to out-rank field work and clinical experience.[14]'

One weakness with this model is that theology becomes too academic oriented and hardly makes sense to the grassroot church communities. Training becomes too skewed towards theory and unfortunately, the practical aspects of ministry tend to be neglected. Also, spiritual

---

[14]'How then shall we train?' Unpublished lecture given to the faculty of Union Biblical Seminary, Poona, Jan 1984.

formation of individual trainees often suffer because, although the theology faculties intend to influence the university in a more Christian way, the university culture and spirit of 'unlimited freedom' in all sorts of directions prove much stronger in shaping a more influential culture that are not always 'Christian' in such areas as work ethics, personal relations, moral principles and standards.

The impact of graduate school model is that often in an effort to gain 'university acceptance and 'academic standards' or credibility; relevance and practical applicability is sacrificed as scholars retreat into academic ivory towers and loose touch with realities on the pastoral front that they are supposed to serve. One way to address this challenge is to seek to adopt a hybrid of two models: 'the graduate school model' and what we introduced a few paragraphs earlier, the 'project model.' My proposal here is that, while retaining the best of the graduate model, there is need to emphasis internship and practical placements much more than school-based residential learning. In effect we are advocating an introduction of 'learning theology by apprenticeship' a kind of modification of what now exists as Theological Education by Extension in many African contexts. A similar model is what Charles Fielding called the professional model. He explains this model in the following words:

> that ministers are professionals among professionals, that the theological curriculum needs to be shaped by the realities of ministerial practice, that theological education, while still based on acquiring knowledge from the full academic range of theological studies, is primarily concerned with producing professional church leaders, and that educational standards, pastoral competency, and personal growth need to be measured. How were such standards, competency and growth to be measured? Not by a traditional diet of lectures and exams, but by new initiatives that included clinical pastoral education, supervised field placements, action/reflection exercises, and case-study methods.[15]

---

[15]http://goliath.ecnext.com/coms2/gi_0199-4190911/Where-do-ministers-come-from.html.

We need new models of theological education where academically qualified theologians can prove effective and useful in the academy as well as at the grass root pastoral setting. A theological educator must be able to publish in referred journals and gain academic credibility, but at the same time should be capable of holding audience with street children, prisoners, lawless gangs and can conduct bible studies among the prostitutes, drug addicts and others of such similar estate. We can do ourselves a lot of good if only we can run away from a scenario that is becoming too common: "that theology is taught by highly intelligent scholars who have spent more of their lives in the library than in the street."[16] This unfortunate scenario tends to forget that a credible and meaningful theology is often a product of engagement with the people and arises out of deep reflection on a concrete pastoral situation.

The Academic or Curricular Model
Another type of the western theological model is one based on the curriculum. A survey of several curricula of theological institutions in Africa confirms that most institutions have a sevenfold division of subject areas, modeled on the western traditional curriculum both in terms of structure and content. The divisions include: Biblical Studies, Theology and Philosophy, Ecclesiastical History, Liturgy, Religion Studies (sometimes including Missiology), Practical and Pastoral Studies, and Ethics or Moral Theology.[17] In the classical curriculum the areas of study are organized simply into four departments of exegetical (biblical), historical, systematic, and practical theology.[18] The degrees at which the 'inherited' curriculum

---

[16]Michael C. Griffiths, "Theological Education Need Not be Irrelevant," *Vox Evangelica* 20 (1990): 7-20.

[17]Joseph Galgalo and Esther Mombo, "Theological Education and Ecumenical Formation: Some Challenges," *Ecumenical Formation* July/October 2002 vol.98/99, 7-14.

[18]For a detailed treatment of this subject see Richard A Muller, *The Study of Theology: From Biblical Interpretation to Contemporary Formulation* (Grand Rapids, Michigan: Zondervan, 1991).

model is contextualized differ from one institution to another. With regard to theological education in the Southern region of Africa, for example, Paul H Gundani et al. write that,

> "The history of theological education in the region has basically been characterized by foreignness, that is, foreign theological content, methodology and languages... Theological education in the region has been captive to the North Atlantic worldview, and is showing little signs of struggle out of this form of oppression."[19]

Gundani's view generally expresses the truth of western models as the dominant models for teaching of theology in most parts of Africa. The use of the Western theological models may be problematic but are not without mitigating factors. A few of such reasons could be mentioned:

> "Confessional reasons and conservatism that prefers the status quo, lack of expertise, and not least, lack of vision, and absence of dynamic leadership. While these are 'internal' or 'African' factors, there also are 'external' factors that contribute to the continued use of the 'inherited model.' Lack of resources, especially human, has, for example, made African theological institutions heavily dependent on 'imported' theological teachers.[20] They cannot be blamed for teaching what they know and the way they know it."[21]

Even where theological faculties are well staffed with African teachers, a good number of them are western trained. As Michael C Griffiths observes:

> It is not only that missionary theological educators have carried the virus with them, but that the process of colonization means that

---

[19]"The State of Theological Education in Southern Africa: Issues and Concerns," *Ecumenical Formation* July/October 2002 vol.98/99, 67-75.
[20]ibid, 67.
[21]J. D. Galgalo and G. LeMarquand; eds. *Theological Education in Contemporary Africa* (Eldoret, Zapf Chancery, 2004), 22-23.

Asians, Africans and Latin Americans are forced into the mould of our western theological establishment and if they are to be credible in our terms, then they must first come and study theology in [Western] universities before they are qualified to teach in their own colleges. As Harvie Conn expresses it, 'Third World patterns continue to go to the West for educational circumcision.'[22]

The problem is further compounded by western oriented library resources such as books and research findings, which greatly determine theological orientation, content, sources and methods of how theology is taught in the African institutions. No wonder then that the study of theology in Africa has largely remained 'western' in almost every aspect. One characteristic of the curriculum model is its emphases on distinct content. The goal is to ground the learner in the knowledge of the content taught, which does not necessarily help the learner in spiritual formation, or acquiring and mastering effective ministerial skills. There is also always the gap between theory and application where theories learnt in class are ill suited for the pastoral context in which the practitioner finally operates.

I propose that the content of each subject should be given a practical orientation by the way they are taught. This could be achieved in one simple way. The examination of practical pastoral skills should be made compulsory and that all other aspect of the curriculum should be designed around this goal. Exegesis, for example, should be intermarried with homiletics and principles of interpretation tested in actual concrete situation of preaching or teaching. That way, such subjects usually regarded as theoretical can be translated into practical studies. Also, if 'project model' combined with graduate school model is adopted as the main structural model of theological training, the curriculum will eventually be shaped by questions that arise from the context of practice.

---

[22]Michael C. Griffiths, "Theological Education Need Not be Irrelevant," *Vox Evangelica* 20 (1990): 7-20.

The Hermeneutical Model

Another model that has shaped and continues to influence Africa's theological formation is a model that is basically of a Western hermeneutical type. Historical-critical method of biblical and theological interpretation is one of the dominant western hermeneutical models that have continued to influence hermeneutical methods in Africa. Biblical critical methods largely fail to bridge the world of the reader and that of the author. Even the proponents of these methods now agree that biblical criticism, with its emphasis on neutrality and assumed objectivity is largely unhelpful: Walter Wink argues that biblical criticism is:

> "Bankrupt solely because it is incapable of achieving what most of its practitioners considered its purpose to be: so to interpret the Scriptures that the past becomes alive and illumines our present with new possibilities for personal and social transformation."[23]

This approach, as pointed out, is particularly problematic because of the 'hermeneutical gap' that exists between the world of the writer and that of the reader. By hermeneutical gap we mean that meaning can hardly be transferred between contexts without distortion, modification or reinterpretation. On this account alone, the western theological resources are inadequate to provide answers for questions raised from a totally different context. They are methods that are a product of a different context from that of Africa, borne out of theological reflections inspired by different situations in life and expressed distinctively in the context of that situation. Similarly, the use of historical critical methods as applied to the bible makes it very difficult, if not impossible, to understand or interpret what the text meant then and what it means now. The difficulty to transfer meaning across time and context is what we are here referring to as the hermeneutical gap that exists between these two contexts.

---

[23] *The Bible in Human Transformation* (Fortress Press, 1983), 2.

This difficulty perhaps accounts for the existing dichotomy between the church and the academy, where theories learnt in the academic institutions are hardly applied in the corresponding pastoral settings. Often our graduates of theology are having to learn everything all over again; as soon as they realize what they learned in the seminary or universities hardly work in the pastoral realities in which they find themselves. In such cases, the inevitable gap or disconnect between orthodoxy and orthopraxis cannot be overemphasized. It soon becomes obvious that doctrines as learnt can hardly be integrated into the thought system of the African believer; and so a spontaneous and unguided inculturation takes place as the African Christianity negotiates and renegotiates an amicable accommodation of Christian doctrines alongside practices and believes held from the traditional, cultural and religious world.

The foreignness of the thought forms of western-oriented theology that is taught in Africa raises the questions of effectiveness, relevance and justification of the continued use of western models of theology especially in terms of its content of theological curricula and the methods of delivery. We must note that there are African theologians, churches and theological institutions that are currently doing their best in addressing the situation. There is now increasingly a growing Africanization of the curriculum, human resources, and with it, theological references that engage with the African situation. The example of St. Paul's University that I mentioned above is one such case in point.

One way to strengthen this encouraging development is to adapt what I have called the 'project model,' which simply means conducting theological training as an on-going, open ended, context oriented, lifelong engagement that can be carried in the context of both the academy but more so in the field. The learner is placed in an actual pastoral context for most of the time and continuously engages with live theological and pastoral issues. He or she should have periods of residential training with opportunities to engage with 'conversational partners,' with whom theological discourses and dialogues can be conducted; and as a result theology is formulated.

There should be a seamless interaction between the academy and the context of practice; such that theology can be produced with an eye on the traditional sources (the Bible; the Fathers, etc) on one hand, and the practical context on the other. The learning process should not be governed by timeframes and rigid structures; but by continuous rhythm of residential learning and a longer series of field engagements; a circle that may be followed for as long as this is possible. The model may prove costly but it will be worth its keep.

What is the Future of Western Theological Models in the African Context?

Globalization, and more so, the universality of Christ makes it imperative for mutual sharing and exchange across Christian contexts. There is a lot that the church in the global South can learn from the church in the global North, and mutual exchange and partnership should be encouraged. However, critical application and adoption of models and methods across contexts is imperative. Every context is unique and so is Africa. There are models, be it of structural nature, curricular, or hermeneutical nature that we may adopt but only on the basis of such models' applicability and appropriateness.

We also need to realize that every theology is after all 'contextual' and that we must develop models that are capable of producing meaningful theology of life for each of our contexts. Because of the mitigating factors as discussed above, some of the western models may be here to stay, and so what perhaps needs to be emphasized is that, whatever models may be used, theological studies will be more effective and relevant if undertaken as a life-long learning project; a reflective practice that learns from its authentic sources but lives for its context.

Contextualization: Theology for God's People

African theology in its short history has continued to rapidly evolve from one stage of development to another. Each stage is marked by a distinctive approach or a theological model that seeks ways in which Christianity can be translated into the African context. Looking at the history of the beginning and development of ACT we can clearly see how context has had a great bearing on the way Africans theologize. Three clear phases can be mapped:

> In its early years of development (the 1950s to 1970s), African Christian Theology was mainly a 'reactionary' theology. It was born in the context of colonialism, a context in which majority of African Christians suffered discrimination, exploitation and oppression. Theological formulation became mainly a critique of these situations. Generally, 'western' Christianity was seen as imperialistic and its theology irrelevant for the African context. It was seen as asking questions which were not particularly addressing African concerns or busy providing answers to questions Africans were not asking. This stage gave rise to distinctive calls for adaptation, and indigenization of theology and the Africanization of the church. It is notable that the visible culmination of this stage was perhaps the moratorium debate, where Africanists advocated the withdrawal of foreign missionaries from African mission fields. These were the concerns, for example, of almost all the African Christian conferences that took place between 1960 and 1980, especially among the Protestant churches. Key among these were perhaps the 1962 first International Conference of Africanists in Accra, Ghana; the 1975 Conference on Christianity in Independent Africa, which was held in Jos, Nigeria; and the 1976 Ecumenical Dialogue of Third World Theologians, which was held in Dar-es-Salaam, Tanzania.

The *second* stage was mainly that of inculturation. How can Christianity be made genuinely African and translated into an authentic African Christian faith? Inculturation, to use Justin Ukpong's helpful definition, is "re-thinking and re-expressing the ... Christian message ... [with the intention to integrate] faith and culture and from it is born a new theological expression that is African and Christian."[24] Alongside inculturation, liberation is another model that has proved effective in addressing the situation of marginalization

---

[24]Cited in Emmanuel Martey, *African Theologies*, 1993, 72.

and political oppression and especially the questions of black power, black dignity, identity, as well as issues of social and political justice. It is a theological discourse born in the context of neo-colonialism, dictatorial regimes, oppressive governance, social inequality and injustice, but especially in response to apartheid in the case of the South Africa situation. A type of liberation theology worth mentioning is the African feminist or women theologies whose theological agenda is mainly that of justice and gender equity.

The *third* stage is that of a theological quest that tries to go beyond liberation and inculturation models. One such approach is that of the theology of reconstruction, mainly associated with the Kenyan theologian J. N. K. Mugambi and the South African theologian Villa-Vicencio. Reconstruction models address the question of the task of theology in the context of the post-independent Africa and largely struggle with such issues as civil and political strife, poverty and foreign debt, diseases, HIV, and AIDS.

While the development of African Christian theology is impressive as outlined above, we make two observations. First, despite such significant developments and extraordinary efforts by theologians in proposing appropriate models and influencing the agenda and methods of African theology, African Christianity has largely remained in a deeply enculturated western mold. This is a verdict that the proposed models are simply academic and have not been tried and tested for use in an actual context, or perhaps it could be the case that they are inadequate altogether. Secondly, the models of adaptation, indigenization, inculturation, liberation and even Africanization each narrowly focuses on a particular aspect of Christianity. They are unnecessarily circumscribed and to some extent become inadequate or even confusing if each is applied one in isolation from the other.

In my view, all these terms can be treated under one broad umbrella, that of contextualization. Strictly speaking, all theology is contextual because it takes elements from the context, which then determines theological agenda and method as context at the same time also becomes the hermeneutical tool for interpreting a given theological claim or supposition. Contextualization as a theological category or model takes seriously not only the culture and social realities but also the whole of human experiences and situations, forces and impact of change, issues of political justice and economic realities, religious beliefs and practices. A theology that is grounded in the context of practice is also bound to be fruitful in one other way; determining the most appropriate method.

One weakness common to all models proposed for the study of theology in the African context lies with the proposed models themselves. The models are all too dogmatic in the sense that they prescribe what needs to be done. A good example is the case of inculturation. In this model, elements from culture are identified and employed as a hermeneutical key to understand the African worldview as well as the interpretation of the bible. The approach is bound to fail because 'prescription' eventually imposes that which is prescribed. The best way to formulate a contextually relevant theology is to tap into a theology that naturally arises in response to the gospel message. The emergent contextual theology is likely to be successful and can be systematized, evaluated for its orthodoxy and credibility and guided through the channels in which such theology has already found local or indigenous expressions. A good example is the Christian doctrine of God, which we present here as one example though only briefly.

The Doctrine of God: A Sketch

One way of looking at theology is that, theology is an interrogation of the nature of God and of how God is known and related to. My working definition of theology is that theology is a systematic ordering of beliefs and practices that arise from the expression of a religious faith. Theology as an academic discipline involves deep reflection upon matters of faith and cogent articulation of the meaning, purpose and place of the whole of creation in relation to the creator. Revelation is the primary source of our knowledge of God, and theologizing, therefore, involves telling the story of our divine encounter or experiences of revelation. In the Christian tradition, the scripture is the primary witness to the revelation of God, in which God is the agent of self-revelation without which God cannot be known. Based on this witness God is specifically revealed as triune. How best can we articulate this fact of divine revelation for the African context?

Maybe, if first things be said first, we may need to ask: do we even need to teach or articulate such a doctrine for the African context? Is it not enough that Africans belief in God, and that the exact detail of the nature of this doctrine is indeed irrelevant for everyday life? Any doctrine can be said to be irrelevant to everyday life only if it is misunderstood or not understood at all. Any doctrine, in as far as such is based on revelation, is practical and relevant. It is also true to say that theology or doctrine is not incomprehensible but theologians often are. On the relevancy of the doctrine of Trinity, for example, how best can we understood trinity in the African context?

"The God who reveals himself according to scripture is One in three distinctive modes of being subsisting in their mutual relations as the Father, Son and the Holy Spirit."[25] Modes of being, persons, *ousia* or *substantia* are categories that down the centuries have provided linguistic frame for Trinitarian expressions for the Christian tradition. The western theological framework is here informed by the rich Greek philosophical tradition. Even, with such helpful philosophical frame of reference it has not been easy to unpack satisfactorily the Trinitarian mystery of God who reveals himself as "One in three related beings.' The expression definitely requires a translation into an African mode of thought. This is where context can aid our frame of thought for a theological articulation that is relevant and understandable.

African worldview is theocentric. God is at the centre of every existence and without God nothing can exist. This provides as with a helpful theoretical framework. In this regard, God reveals himself as a relational being and is capable of expressing his presence in infinitely different ways. The concept of relational nature of every

---

[25]Karl Barth, *Church Dogmatics*, 1/1, 348.

existent is at the heart of the African view of life and that of the cosmic reality within which a person finds oneself. The view is best summed up in the basic philosophy that, "because I relate therefore I am."[26] The reality of existence is in its interconnectedness conceived as a kind of life-force which pervades the whole of nature. The idea of existence in total independence as an individual entity complete in oneself is inconceivable. Kinship is the basic point of African relational interconnectedness. It is the context within which the meaning of life and the whole of existence is summed up. This is an elaborate system within which lineage, family, clan and community forms the basic facets of the communal existence within which an individual finds identity, belonging and the fullness of being or completeness as a person. God, the origin and the sustainer of all existence is thus understood in Africa as relational in nature; for God is the very existence and to exist is to relate. Since God is eternal, he must possess a relational nature, otherwise how could god have been in existence before any other existence came into being? The African belief in God is set in the context of a worldview that conceives the nature of God as relational in and of himself, intimating an existence of relational interconnected modes within one God. Biblical revelation simply comes onto such a context and puts a name to each mode as Father, Son and the Holy Spirit.

Explain the Trinity in such a way is not simply an academic exercise without practical value. Understanding of God as relational and triune has enormous practical implications for every day life. The doctrine of trinity demonstrates that life is 'life-in-relationship,' first in relationship with God, who being the cause of every existence relates to each part of creation as its source. Secondly, life is life-in-relationship with the whole of God's creation to which we are connected by virtue of our connection with God through whom we are brought into inseparable interconnectedness with all. The very idea of separation or individualism among African people is perceived

---

[26]J. S. Mbiti, *African Religions and Philosophy* (Garden City, New York: Doubleday and Company, 1970), 1.

as antithetical to life. The underlying philosophy here is: "In Africa becoming a 'person', that is, a responsible complete subject, is not an individualistic act, but a common project, the relationship of a commitment of solidarity in being-in-history to those who share the same becoming."[27] The whole of reality is one, where ideally all share in a common belonging for the express purpose of communion and harmonious existence. Accepting that the whole of life is 'life-in-relation' is to accept that we cannot be without God the very basis of our existence, and that our relationship with God informs all our other relationships. We can truly say, 'I am because you are,' only if we can first say, 'I am because God is.' The logic here is that God being eternal, everything else must be derivative from God either in the mediate or direct sense because God alone has always been in existence.

Conclusion

What should be the way forward for how theology can best be done in Africa? How can theology be made truly contextual and credible and Christianity truly transformative? What is needed is an infusion of concrete pastoral experience and an academic rigor that generates a reflective theology that can do justice to the traditional sources of God's revelation of himself and the contextual realities into which God speaks to us and encounters humanity today. In practice this should involve a restructuring of the structural model where great emphasis should be laid on experiential learning (placements) than residential school – and that theological education becomes a lifelong learning project. In achieving this goal, what is expected of the theological students should also be demanded from the lecturers who teach theology. They too must have equal or even larger doses of pastoral experience. Theological learning and applicability can only be more effective if the lectures became

---

[27]"Jesus in the Village," in Robert Schreiter, *Faces of Jesus in Africa* (Orbis, Maryknoll, 2002), 34.

facilitators and 'conversational partners' and not 'knowledge dispensing 'demi-gurus.'

Relating theological ethics and doctrines to actual practical pastoral context is bound to encourage reflective 'theologizing.' Such theological exercise and training is the key to our realization of transformative Christianity that can shape a liberating social model and just humanity. With relevant theological education, we can also begin to address the paradoxes that lie at the heart of African Christianity, which we expounded in chapter one. There are, however, emergent forms of African Christianity that cannot be ignored. The emerging patterns are beginning to shape the future directions of Christianity in Africa. We now turn to explore this, in the next chapter.

CHAPTER FOUR

African Christianity: Prospects and New Directions

Introduction

In chapter one, we canvassed possible reasons for the superficiality of 'African Christianity.' In chapters two and three, we proposed mission and theological education as two possible solutions to addressing many disconnects at the heart of 'African Christianity.' In the present chapter, we explore new trends and directions and ask if Pentecostalism is the emerging face of 'African Christianity.' In this regard, African Christianity is finding and domiciling new ways of Christian expressions and teachings that resonate with the prevailing social realities.

Is Christianity Too Heavenly Oriented and Largely Irrelevant for Life Here and Now?

There is an old sentiment that Christianity is often too heavenly oriented to the point of being earthly useless. Too much of worldly concern is believed to provide a foothold for the devil. Consequently, Christians often in an effort to flee from the corrupting world, "lose interest in their earthly tasks, since preoccupation with the absolute has left no place for the ephemeral, the contingent, and the temporal."[1]

---

[1]Gustavo Gutierrez, "Toward a Theology of Liberation" (July 1968), translated by Alfred T Hennelly, (ed). *Liberation Theology: A Documented History* (NY: Orbis, 1990), 66.

This is also the Marxist critique of Christianity: that Christians, with their ambivalent, almost negative attitude to the world, there is something contradictory in their general orientation and attitude. The perceived contradiction seemingly arises when, "often Christians, with their gaze fixed on the world beyond, manifest little or no commitment to the ordinary life of human beings."[2]

Christianity cannot really be said to be inherently 'other worldly.' Such sentiment can perhaps only reflect a deficiency or shortcomings of sorts in practice. Admittedly, a situation of disinterest in these worldly affairs among the religious often can result, due to the lack of a holistic religious approach in executing the mission of the church. Such approach unfortunately ends up compartmentalising human needs into spiritual and physical boxes, or sacred and secular pursuits where one is emphasised in serious neglect of the other. The naturalistic worldview so nurtured by the Enlightenment, with the supernatural largely disregarded has not helped matters either. One of the legacies of the Enlightenment is that it sowed seeds of great confidence in human progress. The Enlightenment culture nurtured the belief that there was no limit to what humanity could achieve in literature, art, architecture, science and technology. As the belief in infinite human potential took to the centre stage of human thought and life, religion increasingly became marginalized, thus making God largely irrelevant or a matter of private affair to be held separate from public life.

With the Enlightenment, as Colin Brown succinctly describes, "what has happened is that man has become more rational. He has thrown off outmoded beliefs. He has rejected, if not God, then at least the ritual and paraphernalia of the churches. It is all part and parcel of man coming of age and living a life of his own."[3] The basic contention is of religion's perceived irrelevancy, its impotence in contributing to human progress, and its failure to affirm positive

---

[2]Ibid, 6.
[3]*Philosophy and the Christian Faith* (Leicester: IVP, 1968), 39.

human values in the context of these worldly realities. This was, for example, exactly the misgivings that communism had against Christianity. Engels, one of the communists' leading lights; compares Christianity and socialism in the following words:

> Christianity and socialism proclaim the proximate liberation of humanity from slavery; but Christianity proclaims it in the next life, not here on earth. This is the difference. We are both agreed that humanity has to be liberated; however, for Christians it is later on, while for us it is now.[4]

The critics of religious traditions generally endorse Engels' thesis. It is argued that religion will die a natural death when humanity finally rejects it for what it sees as religion's apparent irrelevance. The critics are convinced that, "many benefits once looked for, especially from heavenly powers, man has now enterprisingly procured for himself."[5] The evidence we have, however, does not support these claims. Most world religions today are not only alive and well, but are also growing vibrantly. It is indeed ironical that communism or Marxism, a one time leading critic with regard to future of religious traditions is itself now faced with a bleak future. As one scholar observes, "perhaps Marxism is alive today only in our academic world."[6] Of course, this is rather exaggerated and we certainly have not seen the last of Communism, China being a case in point. The point we are making is that humanity come of age, has not, as predicted, succeeded in bringing about the demise of religion or redundancy of religious practices. Christianity is one such world religion that is flourishing. It is not only vibrant but also has successfully continued to adapt to changing times, cultures and contexts. In this chapter, we address the question of Christianity's prospects and future.

---

[5]Vatican II, *Gaudium et Spes*, no.33, cited in Alfred T. Hennelley, Op. cit, 67.

[6]Thomas J. J. Altizer, *The Contemporary Jesus* (London, SCM Press, 2010), x.

We shall frame our arguments around the question of why Christianity has continued to attract large following in many parts of the world, and especially Africa. Why has Christianity continued to inspire and transform numerous followers despite such enormous challenges as secularism, scientific progress, and competition from other faiths? What particular motifs and themes make Christianity attractive? What will the shape of future African Christianity look like and what trends, emphases and directions will emerge?

Images of Jesus

Christianity without Jesus the Christ is an unlikely project. Down through the centuries, Jesus has continued to fascinate, inspire, transform, liberate and empower millions. His stories—feeding the hungry, healing the sick, raising the dead and dying to save are simply extraordinary. There is something clearly convincing about Jesus that he was not simply an ordinary man with extraordinary abilities. He is revealed, through his life and ministry, as divine. He does not only have power over life and death but he is the very life. His mission is universal and his love all encompassing. He encounters us though numerous images made manifest in his work. His varied functional roles present him all at once as the bread to the hungry, water of life, shepherd of the soul, Emmanuel, healer, saviour, king and prophet. In Luke 4:18, a passage based on Isaiah's prophecy (61:1-2) and generally interpreted as the messiah's mission statement, Jesus is pictured as a great liberator. This image sums up Jesus' role in human salvation as it is basic to all these other messianic titles and roles. He liberates whether by healing, feeding, raising, empowering or saving.

The image of Jesus-the-liberator has down the centuries been a dominant theological model for various contexts. For example, it could be said to be the primary inspiration for the modern day Latin American liberation theology. The Latin American liberation theology is born out of a context of abject poverty and ineffective socio-economic policies. An appropriate and relevant theology was needed to face the challenge, and this naturally inclined towards the search for human liberation. An image of Jesus that can identify with the peoples' everyday reality, aspirations, and hope, was needed. The Church and her theologians needed to awaken to the realities of the day or else risk being irrelevant.

A few Latin American theologians may be mentioned in this regard. Gustavo Gutierrez is indisputably a pioneer and rightly regarded as the father of modern day Latin American liberation theology. Leonardo Boff and Jon Sobrino, however, are really two authors who have laid a firm foundation for liberation Christology. This is a Christology that places orthopraxis and orthodoxy on equal footing where 'I believe' is necessarily followed by 'I do.' The Christ 'with the poor' provides the departure point for liberation Christology and its basic hermeneutical framework. It is a theological discourse that besides seeking to hold together faith and practice, also demonstrates through discipleship, the relevance of God's liberating grace in specific life situations. This goes to the heart of the primary concern of not only liberation Christology, but the whole of liberation theology. It is worth mentioning that liberation theology succeeded not just as a result of 'image-fixing' ('Christ-as-liberator'). It succeeded as a result of people's obedient response to Christ's call to discipleship.

As Rebecca Chopp aptly summarises, "liberation theology represents a radical engagement of Christianity with the world, with the intent to represent human freedom and God's gratuitous activity in the questions and issues of the day ... liberation theology reflects and guides a Christianity that is identified with those who suffer ..."[7] Jesus-the-liberator, who himself takes sides with the damned of the world and bears their suffering serves a practical purpose in enlivening hope and inspiring actions that relevantly contribute towards the realization of a just society. Believers come to Jesus not as their superhero but as a true liberator who gives them hope, possibilities, and actual liberation from all that dehumanises. Jesus

---

[7]*The Praxis of Suffering: An Interpretation of Liberation and Political Theologies* (Maryknoll, NY: Orbis Books, 1986), 153.

is not just another Hollywood superhuman figure like Spiderman, Batman, or Ironman – who may inspire the possibility of a fusion of the world of reality and fiction. Jesus, on the contrary is real, he is the omnipotent liberator who offers infinite possibilities in overcoming difficulties in this life by giving the power that makes liberation truly possible.

In Africa, as Teresa Hinga observes, "the prevailing image of Christ was that of Christ the conqueror."[8] The theme of liberation, however, despite its socio-political concerns is different from that of the Latin American Liberation theology. It is characteristically shot through with the quest to clarify the African identity, as well as liberate the African person from mental, economic and cultural enslavement in which the African person is consciously or unconsciously trapped as a result of the continued western domination that begun with the colonization of Africa.

In Africa, especially in the South, liberation theology is closely identified with Black theology. In this respect, and perhaps only this, African liberation theology shares close affinity with the American Black theology, which arose out of the context of black response to the paternalistic 'white theology' that generally fostered the image of a 'white supremacist Christ.' Black theology (of whatever geographical context) is a type of liberation theology, with its primary goal as the emancipation of the disempowered person. As Emmanuel Martey, puts it, black theology is "the quest for anthropological dignity."[9] It is a quest for the liberation of the whole person (physical, psychological and spiritual) from all that oppresses and or hinders the realization of God given potential to enjoy the abundance of life that Christ the liberator gives.

---

[8]Teresa M. Hinga, "Jesus Christ and the Liberation of Women in Africa," in Mercy Amba Oduyoye and Musimbi R. A. Kanyoro (eds.) *The Will to Arise* (Maryknoll, NY: Orbis, 1992), 187.

[9]*African Theology: Inculturation and Liberation* (Maryknoll, NY: Orbis, 1993), 96.

Black theology, following in the footsteps of Liberation Theology, draws its hermeneutical inspiration from the Exodus motif of 'bondage' and 'delivery' or liberation. Its praxis is inspired by the life, ministry and teaching of the historical Jesus who personally entered into human history and shared the predicament of the despised of the earth. Jesus becomes the perfect model of one who experienced the very depth of humiliation, suffering and death, and yet emerged victorious. He is the liberator who releases from bondage of all forms and leads into freedom and the fullness of life.

The 'liberator model' or Jesus Christ the liberator is an image that speaks directly into the African context. Given the inspiration that this dominant image affords, Christianity cannot surely be accused of irrelevance or of being 'other worldly.' For being in grips with the realities of human need in the here and now, Christian faith is undoubtedly capable of eliciting what Teresa Hinga called "the emancipatory impulses."[10] In this regard, we observe that liberation, abundance of life, healing and salvation form the core emphases, themes and motifs of African Christianity today. The image of "Christ the liberator ... [first] found expression in missionary praxis."[11] This was more by default than design. When the poor, the oppressed and the disempowered encounter Jesus through the gospel stories, they find a powerful ally who fills them with hope. They see in Jesus one who having walked a similar path of life of hardship, identifies with them, and now leads all who follow him to their true destiny, that is, a place and status of ultimate victory and liberation. Pentecostalism is one brand of Christianity in Africa today that greatly emphasises this theme. They are among the churches that in using this model of Christ the liberator, have continued to register enormous successes in attracting following.

---

[10] Op. cit, 189.
[11] Teresa Hinga, ibid, 188-9.

Pentecostalism: The Christianity of the Future?[12]

Pentecostalism is a general term loosely applied to a number of Christian denominations. A clarification of how we have used this term is here in order. In its general use the term usually refers to a renewal movement going back to the Topeka, Kansas incident of 1901, reportedly triggered by a unique experience of believers who claimed of being filled with the Holy Spirit. The movement has since become a major segment in Christianity adapting the descriptive name Pentecostalism, to distinguish itself from Roman Catholicism and the Protestant churches that historically go back to the Reformation. Pentecostalism is distinct from charismatic and neo-Pentecostal (also called 'third-wavers') groups. These groups are found within the first and second 'waves' of Christianity (that is, Catholicism and Protestantism respectively). The actual Pentecostals (also called classical or mainline Pentecostals) are also of various orientations and carry varied thematic emphases despite their basic similarities.

The majority of the classical Pentecostals ascribe to a similar theological and doctrinal outlook. The most notable of this is the belief in a necessary post-conversion experience involving baptism in or with the Holy Spirit. The centrality of the Bible is endorsed, and like most evangelistically oriented Protestant churches, salvation through faith in Christ alone is also affirmed. For the classic Pentecostals, however, some form of manifestation of the gifts of the Spirit is required as a sure sign of a regenerate life. The gift of either *glossolalia* or *xenolalia* (either one alongside the other or one as alternative to the other) is especially emphasised in this regard. Note that *glossolalia* and *xenolalia* are different. *Glossolalia* is the

---

[12]Philip Jenkins in his book, *The Next Christendom*, [(Oxford: OUP), 2002] provides us with a lucid and thorough analysis of what he called in his sub-title, "*the coming of global Christianity*." I am indebted to this work for most of my insights in this section, especially on statistics and the reasons for the rapid worldwide growth of the Pentecostal churches.

gift of speaking in strange, unknown tongues, and *xenolalia*, also referred to as *xenoglossia* is the gift or ability to speak in one or many identifiable foreign languages without prior exposure to such a language.

Despite these similarities, Pentecostals do have their points of theological differences. This includes, for example, teachings on either the two-stage way or three-stage way of salvation, the nature and working of sanctification, or even the doctrine of the trinity, which although accepted by majority of the Pentecostal Churches, is not ascribed to, for instance, by the Oneness Pentecostals. These differences have resulted into divisions, and today different Pentecostal denominations are estimated at over 12,000.[13]

The Pentecostal Churches' diversity is also reflected in the Kenyan Pentecostalism, which includes such denominations as the Church of God, Kenya Assemblies of God, the Full Gospel Churches, Pentecostal Assemblies of God, Pentecostal Evangelical Fellowship of Africa and numerous home-grown Pentecostals such as the Redeemed Gospel and Deliverance Churches. On account of their basic similarities, theological outlook, and their approach to evangelism; we shall use the term Pentecostalism in a general sense and treat these churches together except where specific examples are in view.

The phenomenal growth of Christianity in the whole of the third world is well documented. Philip Jenkins observes, that in Africa, for example, "a period of explosive growth [beginning with the end of colonialism] still continues unchecked." Quoting from the 2001 edition of the *World Christian Encyclopedia*, he points out that "The Present net increase on that continent [Africa] is 8.4 million new Christians a year (23,000 a day), of which 1.5 million are new

---

[13]Russell P Spittler, "Children of the Twentieth Century," in Robin Keeley (org. ed.), *The Quiet Revolution* (Oxford: Lion Publishers), 1985, 77 cp. *Dictionary of Pentecostal and Charismatic Movements* eds. Stanley M. Burgess and Gary B. McGee, (Grand Rapids: MI:, 1988), 811.

converts ..."[14] He also notes that "In recent years, some of the most successful congregations have been Pentecostal ..."[15] and that "In most of Africa, Pentecostals have overtaken the independent or indigenous churches in popularity."[16]

Aylward Shorter and Joseph Njiru, writing from the Kenyan context reveal a similar trend. They agree that, "Pentecostalism is a major force on the religious scene of Kenya today."[17] A comparison that they make between the growth of the Pentecostal churches and the 'mainline' Protestant churches is revealing. Basing their analysis on a 1986 survey of the churches in Nairobi, they observe that: "mainline Pentecostals in the city had already over taken Anglicans and Presbyterians in numbers, and that there was one Pentecostal for every Catholic." They also make a reasonable guess that "this figure has probably trebled in the intervening fifteen [or so] years."[18] In the light of this numerical success, it is obvious that Pentecostalism is today, the dominant type of Christianity that seems to attract greater following and growing faster than the rest of the denominations. An important observation is that a great majority of the Pentecostal members is composed of those abandoning their traditional denominations. We must, however, be quick to add that this does not mean that the non-Pentecostal, traditional Christianity is necessarily facing extinction. What mission strategies, themes or emphases are contributing to the success of Christianity but more specifically to the phenomenal growth of the Pentecostal Churches?

Heavenly Vision for Earthly Glory: The 'Faith-Gospel' Doctrine

Harvey Cox, the author of the celebrated book on Pentecostalism, *Fire from Heaven* (1995), puts economics and generally the promise

---

[14]Op. cit, 56.

[15]ibid, 68.

[16]ibid, 68.

[17]*New Religious Movements in Africa* (Nairobi: Pauline Publications, 2001), 26.

[18]ibid, 29.

of well being at the heart of the new mission strategies and directions. He aptly summarises this in the following words:

> "Money – why you don't have enough and how to get more – has come to play such a central role in many Pentecostal churches that recently a whole new theology has grown up around it. It is premised on the belief that God not only wills eternal life for all believers, but robust health and material prosperity as well. They call it "the-health-and-wealth gospel.""[19]

Philip Jenkins, explaining the reasons for success of the churches in the 'two-thirds world,' or the 'South' as he prefers to call them, says that "the various Southern churches are growing in response to ... economic circumstances. Their success can be seen as a by product of modernization and urbanization."[20] In the quickly changing social settings, economic hardships, and where success is largely controlled by means of cut-throat competitions between different production systems, people often experience alienation, and a high degree of vulnerability. Jenkins observes that "In such settings, the most devoted and fundamentalist-oriented religious communities emerge to provide functional alternative arrangements for health, welfare, and education."[21] The churches usually present themselves as an avenue or place where the uprooted or socially alienated rural immigrants can belong and redefine or 'discover' anew, their identities. The church structures, so to speak, provide 'functional equivalents' to social and communal structures that crumble, or which the alienated are forced to leave behind. The alternative or new structures greatly bear on the identity and self-motivation of the individual.

The Church leadership and the fellowship of support communities, are a part of the means of reordering ones life, in semblance of what one already know, yet liberating, as an alternative

---

[19] Harvey, Cox *Fire From Heaven* (Reading: Massachusetts, Perseus Books, 1995), 271.
[20] Op. cit, 72-3.
[21] ibid, 73.

and perceivably affording a better arrangement. At some levels there is the perception that a church that adequately meets this need empowers and so becomes means to liberation—from all that alienates and threatens the attainment of one's fullness of being, the realization of personal potential and one's aspirations as a social being. These churches succeed as long as the social and spiritual needs of the members are met. The services that these churches provide, among other things, include 'social security' through fellowship that affords networking with people, which if managed well, in turn ensures a sustained growth.

While this is generally true for any church, it is particularly the case for most of the Pentecostal churches. Indeed it has been observed that the Pentecostal churches, particularly in their beginnings characteristically attract the poor, vulnerable and marginalized groups of people. This can be verified from the historical beginnings of most Pentecostal churches. Nils Bloch-Hoell, for example, writing with regard to the social composition of the members of the early Pentecostal movements in England, cites an example of the Church of God in Birmingham. He records that the greater percentage of the initial members "were poor from the humble walks of life. Many were common labourers and farmers, with very limited education …"[22] He also points out that a similar kind of pattern, with regard to the social status of the Pentecostal adherents, is usually repeated from place to place. Norway is a case in point. "The Pentecostal Movement in Norway was supported by the lower ranks of society than by the average Norwegian."[23]

Numerous such other examples can be cited. Jenkins points out that "Pentecostalism in Latin America has appealed particularly to the very poorest groups, such as Brazil's Black population and Mexico's Mayan Indians, who find in the churches a real potential

---

[22] *The Pentecostal Movement: Its Origin, Development and Distinctive Character* (London: Allen & Unwin, 1964), 172.
[23] ibid, 172.

for popular organization."[24] In Africa too, the Pentecostal churches attract mainly the marginalized and vulnerable group of people—especially the women, unemployed and the young who are in constant search for fulfilment and success in life. Bloch-Hoell's conclusion is as true for Africa as it is for his case studies that "The Pentecostal Movement still lacks university-trained ministers, scholarly theology, liturgical tradition ..."[25] which is a true reflection on the social standings of the majority of its adherents. In Kenya, we have a good example of people from humble social backgrounds rising to the helm of the leadership of one or the other of the Pentecostal churches, or founding some of the most successful congregations in Kenya today.[26]

The fact of the Pentecostal members' general background is an indication that the kind of Christianity at work in these churches is not at all 'a pie in the sky' or about a paradise that simply lies somewhere in the realm of life after death. It is a Christianity that through its distinctive thematic emphases has succeeded in providing a practical setting where people can improve their daily living here and now. This happens when the church is able to "provide channels of mobility"[27] either through social projects, or by way of its preaching and doctrinal emphasis, that can influence the believers' way of thinking, their attitudes to life, commitment, and determination to realize the abundant life that the gospel promises. The key to the realization of this goal is of course faith in Jesus Christ who gives power to overcome all that dehumanises.

Most of the Pentecostal churches in Kenya are young, urban centred, and gives preference to evangelism over social action. It is therefore of a category that 'specialises' in shaping the believers' way of thinking chiefly by the way Jesus Christ is presented, especially in his mighty liberating role. A recasting of the image of

---

[24]op. cit, 74.
[25]Op. cit, 172.
[26]Cp. Some of the examples cited in Shorter and Njiru, Op. cit, 35.
[27]Philip Jenkins, op. cit, 74.

'Jesus mighty liberator' occurs at the level of evangelism. Emphases are nearly wholly on the blessings in every area of life—especially wealth and health, which are the two strongest points of 'Faith Gospel' doctrine. The 'Faith Gospel' approach characteristically reinterprets salvation as God's blessing, conceived primarily in terms of this earthly glory, equated with the biblical idea of the 'abundance of life,' which comes with the freedom from the encumbrances of poverty and ill-health. Such freedom is typically described in language such as breakthrough or release by the power of faith in Jesus.

The 'Faith Gospel,' also popularly referred to as 'the Prosperity Gospel' invokes Christ as the saviour who 'liberates' from the malignant spirits bent on robbing the believers' 'claim' to the fullness of life. The liberator Christ gives the 'power' to counteract especially two of such malignant spirits, that of 'poverty' and the 'spirit of sickness.' Salvation is not just something acquired now, only to be enjoyed when one gets to heaven. The heavenly vision is rather to be applied to these worldly realities, and that "faith is expected to lead to real and observable results in this world."[28] Jenkins quoting a commentator on Pentecostal churches in Brazil, states this point clearly:

> "Their main appeal is that they present a God that you can use. Most Presbyterians have a God that's so great, so big, that they cannot even talk with him openly, because he is far away. The Pentecostal groups have the kind of God that will solve my problems today and tomorrow. People today are looking for solutions, not for eternity."[29]

The notion of Christ the liberator has proved very potent in the faith of the believer. By the power of faith, that which is impossible by human power is truly possible by the power of God. The believer need not just tell God of pressing needs but boldly claim whatever

---

[28]ibid, 77.
[29]ibid, 77.

they need in the name of Jesus—and it shall be theirs. "People want prosperity—or at least, economic survival,"[30] and these are to be enjoyed while here on earth. In the words of one Pentecostal pastor, "We have salvation, but salvation is in heaven. We are here on earth. Jesus will come but not yet."[31] The preachers of the 'Faith Gospel' generally utilise the heavenly vision of the world to come, to create a paradise on earth, and lead their followers to believe that it can be achieved in the present world by faith and the victory that Jesus gives. The promise of earthly glory, alongside the assurance of ultimate salvation, has proved extremely attractive in a world where materialism has become a new God. It is indeed, in itself, symptomatic of a highly materialistic society, with religion becoming a tool, where *faith-power* or faith in Christ, has become a means to success that largely gets measured in terms of material gain. Religion here becomes, by this principle, a means of production, and like any other system of production, it also becomes susceptible to misuse and abuse. Promise of miracles and release from all sorts of demonic powers have often been commercialised to the point of duly attracting scandals in some of these churches from time to time.

Most Pentecostal pastors, especially those inclined towards this 'Faith Gospel,' preach and sincerely believe that God blesses them materially, and that there is no limit to the number of ways that God can use to dispense his blessings. I shall here rely again on Jenkins' apposite example of the Brazilian *Igreja Universal do Reino de Deus* (IURD), not least for its relevance to the Kenyan context. The Brazilian Universal Church of God, as it is known in its English translation, was founded by Macedo de Bezerra in 1977, and today commands millions of following. The affluence of the leaders could rightly be attributed to the church's method of evangelism. It sells, for example, "special anointing oil for healing, and television viewers are encouraged to place glasses of water

---

[30]ibid, 77.
[31]ibid, 77.

near the screen so they can be blessed by remote control."³² The church is used to controversies, and perhaps the most damaging of scandals was of when "an embarrassing videotape showed Macedo gloating over his profits, and urging lieutenants to squeeze more out of the flock. When the video was aired, the scandal caused a major setback, and the church's previously astronomical growth faltered."³³ In Kenya too, scandals are not unheard of (for example, cases where the sick have been conned of money in the name of healing especially from HIV and AIDS), but more so, a strong emphasis on the gospel of liberation or real prospects of 'earthly glory' is similarly a reality.

In newspaper article entitled, *"Clerics' Lavish Living,"*³⁴ journalists Joe Ombuor and Philo Ikonya, give revealing descriptions of the lifestyles of some of the leading Pentecostal Pastors in Kenya. I shall briefly highlight three from among those mentioned in that article. The first of these is a Pastor of *"Jesus Celebration Centre,"* in Mombasa. According to the article, this pastor is said to be immensely wealthy and lives in a high-class estate in an affluent part of Mombasa. In the words of these two writers, the pastor is, "A symbol of opulence that is in sharp contrast to the majority of the crowd that makes up his regular audience."³⁵ Another example given in the same article is that of a lady prosperity gospeller based in Nairobi. The authors present her as a model of "what it means to be engulfed in religious power and wealth. Apart from riding in the most stately of limos and living in palatial residence, she is always hedged in by bodyguards in and out of her crowded sermons at Nairobi's Uhuru Park."³⁶ The example of another Pastor of the *"Charismatic Gospel Church,"* in Nairobi is also cited in the article.

---

³²ibid, 65.

³³ibid, 65

³⁴The issue of "Your Weekender Magazine," in *Daily Nation*, Friday, March 19, 1999, p.1. I am indebted to Fr. Shorter and Njiru (Op. cit, 35), who citing this article first drew my attention to it.

³⁵ibid, 1.

³⁶ibid, 1.

The story contends that the pastor is originally from Zimbabwe and ministers to a congregation largely from his native country. It is said of him that "Although this church is small, with a mainly middle class congregation of about 700 loyal followers, the Zimbabwean minister drives a Pajero and lives comfortably in Kileleshwa."[37] [Kileleshwa is one of the upmarket suburbs in Nairobi].

If these stories contain any truth, it indicates that religion can be turned into a formidable tool of economic empowerment here on earth besides just being the way to God and eternal salvation. It is as much a business of this world as it is of the world to come. There is no doubt that Jesus Christ is believed and preached to liberate people from the powers of sin and Satan. There is no confusion, however, of where the emphasis of Pentecostal preachers lie: liberation is first and foremost from the 'spirit of poverty,' sickness and all forms of other deterrents to good life on earth. Ingenious packaging of some Kenyan television programs such as, *"Glory is Here"* explains the point. This is meant to be 'the presence of God' but is really revealing of the reality that operates, at least, at the unreflective level or the followers. For most of the 'Faith Gospel' seekers or even presenters, the 'heavenly glory' is not 'a pie-in-the sky' but inspires real possibility of 'earthly glory.'

The doctrine of "Faith Gospel' is attractive not least perhaps for its simplicity. A believer needs not be poor—poverty can be overcome by *faith-power*, or more precisely, by faith, prayer and the planting of the right kind of seeds, which in due season, God will turn into harvest. If the pastor is blessed by God to acquire wealth, he or she serves a living testimony of what faith can achieve. It is a bad example to the faithful if the minister of a rich God, lives in poverty. This conviction and personal techniques are combined to bring about the desired result, which involves 'moving' the congregation to give generously to support the church's ministry but more so for the givers' own blessing. Joe Ombuor and Philo Ikonya, for example, write of a Kenyan prosperity gospel preacher who

---

[37]ibid, 1.

"has been known to spiritually move his followers to part with anything, including selling their cars and houses to give money to the church." A former member of the church testifies to the verity of this claim: "I have seen people taking loans from their places of work to take money to the church."[38] Cases of individual members offering to the tune of three or more million shillings during a given Sunday service are also cited in the same article.

In the Faith Gospel services, people are routinely led to believe that tithes and offertory are a sort of investment. The same principle of market capitalism is exactly at work here. As Jenkins observes, "Believers are told, in effect, that prayer and giving operate on the same crass principle as secular investment: the more one gives to the church, the more material benefit can be expected in this life."[39] The primary goal here seems to be that of "prosperity and financial breakthrough."[40] The Church facilitates this, by inviting the members to 'receive their miracles'. To quote one Mombasa Pastor, for example, at the end of one of his recent sermons, broadcast on the television, his call to his congregation was, "If you are barren, in flesh or business, come now and stand before this congregation, and receive your deliverance."[41] Another leading Pentecostal television evangelist commonly preaches on the theme of 'blessing.' In a sermon entitled "Purpose of Jesus' Anointing," based on Jesus' mission manifesto of Luke 4, she similarly had a typical ending, characteristic of all these Pentecostal preachers. Perhaps a few of her following words summarises it all: "investment gone down the drain," ... "that is yesterday ... Jesus now says I want to bless you.'"[42]

---

[38] *Daily Nation*, op.cit, 1.
[39] Philip Jenkins, op. cit, 65.
[40] Cp. ibid, 65.
[41] "The Power of the Tongue," A sermon preached at his Mombasa "Jesus Celebration Centre," and broadcast on KTN on Sunday 9, February 2003 at 8.00 am.
[42] KBC –Television broadcast on Saturday, 8 February, 2003 at 8.30 pm. (A repeat programme).

Pentecostalism promises its followers the heaven but also the earth, ingraining in the believers' psyche that it is possible to enjoy the best of both worlds. Their prayer is not so much 'your kingdom come,' but 'and may the rest be given to us as well.' The believers do not have to look up to the saints but have living witnesses whose example they can emulate. These are those Christians who are wealthy, and who through their testimony affirm that success through *faith-power* is possible.

In this light, it is very difficult not to see why people are attracted to Pentecostalism, making it the fastest growing branch of Christianity. The 'Faith Gospel,' however, raises many theological as well as pastoral difficulties. A theology that envisions materialism or personal wealth and physical health as the measure of faith is problematic. If the commonplace maxim: 'faith is the answer' is applied as a rigid theological principle, then the well-off are a living proof that *'faith-power'* works. On the other hand, this negatively reinforces the belief that poverty is simply a visible manifestation of an underlying spiritual malady, namely lack of faith. Also, over-emphasising this worldly prosperity runs the danger of easily loosing sight of that which is of the ultimate significance, namely eternal salvation. The Faith Gospel or the Prosperity Gospel is in this sense weak on eschatology.

Faith Gospel and Its Implications for Eschatology
There is generally a certain paradox at the heart of the message of those Pentecostal Churches, which emphasise the imminence of the Second Coming on one hand, and preach prosperity gospel on the other. Broadly speaking, most Pentecostal denominations have a view of history where the future has a great bearing on the present. Most historical events are viewed as the fulfilment of one or the other of many 'written' or 'inspired' prophecies. Their general view of eschatology also shares a lot in common with the views of many 'evangelical' Christians. Perhaps the only difference arises with most Pentecostal's insistence on the 'out-pouring of the Holy Spirit,' sometimes also seen as 'the second Pentecost experience.' This

doctrine generally is interpreted by most Pentecostals as an outward, observable sign of the imminence of the end-time.

The general key to the doctrine of Pentecostal eschatology is perhaps millennialism. Most Pentecostals are pre-millennialists. They believe that Jesus Christ will return to earth before the onset of the millennial reign mentioned in the book of Revelation (chapter, 20:1-10). Most of the Pre-millennialists also ascribe to either a historicist or futurist perspectives in their interpretations of the book of Revelation. The latter teaches the fulfilment of prophecies as wholly to lie in the future, and the historicist believe that fulfilment will be given to the church within the present historical dispensation. The futurists are also divided into pre-tribulationists and post-tribulationists, two views, which do not agree on whether the rapture of the church will occur after or before the great tribulation. The subtle differences in these views, anyway, hardly play out in any notable details among the different Pentecostal groups. It is rather the basic theme of the imminent return of Christ that generally colours the Pentecostal sermons and teachings across the board. The puzzle is how this theme is accommodated alongside the passionate emphases on 'earthly glory' that we mentioned above.

One of the reasons why Pentecostalism is the fastest growing segment of Christianity today is due to the emphasis that they place on the imminence of the second coming of Christ. Indeed in its provenance, "The Pentecostal Movement arose in an atmosphere of fervent expectation of the second coming of Jesus."[43] The terror of coming judgement, the punishment of the unrighteous, and the glorious hope of the saved, provide the basic theme for their sermons.[44] As Markus Hauser notes, "The cry, 'The bridegroom comes!' is extraordinarily powerful at the present day,"[45] as it was

---

[43]Walter J. Hollenweger, *The Pentecostals* (London: SCM Press, 1972), 415.

[44]D. J. Wilson, "Pentecostal Perspectives on Eschatology," in Stanley M Burgess and Gary B. McGee, (eds.) Op. cit, 267.

[45]Cited in Walter J. Hollenweger, op. cit, 415.

when it was first sounded. This powerful message appeals to most hearers encouraging them to hasten and make amends with their God before the end time is eventually upon them. Logically this leaves very little room for social reforms or other worldly pursuits, and indeed many Pentecostals characteristically prioritise evangelism over social action. That is exactly where the paradox lies.

There is an apparent contradiction when we see this in light of the primary concern of the Faith Gospel preachers, where Christ liberates for 'glory' here and now, as much as liberating for the 'glory' to come. This is another factor, which is equally responsible for the upsurge of Pentecostalism. The paradox can, however, be resolved if one sees these two aspects, not as preached concurrently, but as beginning with one only to end with the other. Hollenweger observes how the Pentecostals when they first begin out, zealously preach the message of end time. Besides their sermons, these are especially reflected in their hymns, bulletins and billboard titles such as 'Maranatha,' 'The Midnight Cry,' 'The End-Time Messenger,' among many such other titles. He also notes that although the belief in the second coming persists, the fervour cools down, and "As each denomination grows older, these titles ... tend to be abandoned."[46]

For most Pentecostals, in any case, the emphasis on the Second Advent is only the beginning point. Even when the message is upheld, its emphasis in the face of continued delay of Parousia cannot be sustained for any meaningful length of time. The Pentecostal Adventists, at least in the early stages of their revival fellowships, downplay the reality of these worldly needs, showing a kind of indifference to the physical problems they experience. They take consolation in believing that the problems of this world are only temporary. It could be said that such a belief "works as a palliative which prevents them from despairing in the wretched circumstances in which they live."[47] In the words of Cox, "the rejection of the seductions of the "boutique culture" is an integral part of what it

---

[46]ibid, 415.
[47]Hollenweger, ibid, 417.

means to walk in the spirit."[48] Understandably, this stage does not last for long as other emphases and themes soon take centre stage. This is where the Faith Gospel messengers take over and provide a theme and emphasis that address the immediate concerns that they face in the meantime.

The Faith Gospel Pentecostals, on the whole, end up downplaying eschatological emphasis of the gospel as they concentrate on propagating a strong realist view of a heaven that can be experienced here and now. The hardships in the present life are not simply to be borne bravely until completely subjected to Christ the liberator, but they can actually be overcome here and now by the faithful through *faith-power*. In a way, eschatology is already realised. The Kingdom of God has already begun, and the reign of Christ who liberates from all sorts of bondage is here. God's liberation and the breaking in of his power on human history is characterised by all sorts of blessings, and especially the blessing of good health and prosperity that his people already enjoy. Evidently, "as social conditions improve the fervent expectation of the second coming disappears."[49] The paradox, however, remains in that, while the belief in the Second Advent is upheld, the possibility of experiencing or enjoying a real foretaste of heaven here on earth becomes a reality and is actually believed to be already happening.

Eschatology in this case, is not simply a belief in the heaven to come and other doctrines of last things. Rather, it entails the affirmation of the reality of heaven without giving up on any part of the earth, and utilising the heavenly vision, not only for the hope of things to come, but of creating its promised glory here on earth. In a way, judgement has also begun because the spiritual depravity of the worldly people and the hopelessness of the poor and sick, are a sign of lack of faith, which causes suffering as a logical consequence of 'spiritual poverty' or 'poor spiritual condition.' This last point is ridden with all sorts of moral and theological difficulties. Whereas

---

[48]Harvey Cox, op. cit, 120.
[49]ibid, 417.

we cannot reduce the cause of suffering to some deficient rigid theological principle, on the whole, a doctrine of eschatology that brings the future to bear on the present and thereby delivers the hope of personal, communal and social transformation is to be commended.

Future Directions: "Nothing Sells Like God"
Going by current trends that we have broadly delineated above, Pentecostalism is strongly shaping the future directions of the church in Africa. We may fault its approach and content of mission on a score or two but the Pentecostal brand of Christianity certainly affords invaluable insights and practical lessons for church growth. The Pentecostals' impact on the rest of the universal church of Christ cannot be ignored. The spread of neo-Pentecostalism and charismatic movements, (the so called 'third wavers') within the mainline churches is radically re-shaping the 'traditional' churches. not simply a response to contain Pentecostalism on the part of the traditional ('mainline') churches but a true indication of the future of our Christianity. A number of things could be pointed out as an offering from the Pentecostals to the whole universal church of Christ. Some of such offerings if adopted by other churches will greatly help in shaping the future directions.

In an article, "Make a Million by Hook or Crook," a Kenyan columnist Oyunga Pala suggests twelve different ways in which one can make quick money in Kenya today. One of his twelve suggestions is to "start a church." He aptly summarises the commercialisation of Faith Gospel and of how it works for those who venture into it for business.

> "Nothing sells like God. The key word in this business is miracles galore. Promise fast, painless cures to people with terminal illnesses, using your bare hands and of course the power of the divine working through you."[50]

---

[50] *Saturday With The Nation*, February 15-21, 2003, 8.

Prosperity Gospel has shown that "nothing sells like God." While Pentecostalism generally attributes its phenomenal success in terms of numerical growth to the 'work of the Holy Spirit,' the method of presentation indeed accounts for the numerical successes of these churches more than any other factor. The most successful of the Pentecostal evangelists are those who ably identify and deliver a product that meets real need. The resultant numerical and spiritual growth instinctively becomes motivational for the evangelists. If capitalism, as a system of production has proved the most successful in comparison to others, it is not surprising that Pentecostalism too is succeeding because the same 'general principle' is here applied. The lesson here is that the gospel has real power to unlock potentials for individuals and for effecting the transformation of societies. Faith in God, enlightens, inspires, sustains hope, and affords the satisfaction that, 'in God all is possible.' The whole church of Christ could learn from the Pentecostals' dynamic approach to preaching with passion, relevance and clarity to the point that the hearer may be touched and say, 'yes, this speaks to me.' The thing here is that the message of the gospel must be packaged in ways that is relevant and ways that can directly speak to the hearers' circumstances and real life situations.

We must, however, point out that it will be extremely reductionistic to assume that 'right packaging' is the only factor that accounts for the growth of Pentecostalism. It will be wrong, for example, to assume that all Pentecostals are totally this worldly in orientation and that the sole motivation of every evangelist is out to con his or her followers without exception. The niche on which their 'ecclesiastical market' is built is not just exploited and jealously guarded, but is also spiritually nourished on the word of God. Pentecostal preachers certainly offer, at least at best, the potential for the capacity to engage meaningfully with God and the existential questions of ultimate meaning, purpose of life, and fulfilment. This, I recommend, as the second key lesson all churches could learn from Pentecostal churches. One sure way of growing the church is through meaningful, sustained, biblically based spiritual nourishment of the believers. Great dividends stand to be gained if sound doctrine is deliberately made part of the 'package.'

Spiritual nurture aside, perhaps the greatest credit to be given to Pentecostalism is that of positive attitude to the world. The message of *'faith-power'* carries the capacity to build the believer's self confidence, and the courage to venture out and try things, to better ones life, and live life in all its fullness. To put it in a typical Pentecostal phrase, every believer has the potential 'to be the person that God wants him or her to be.' This has great potential for transformation, both at societal and personal levels. The lesson here, in terms of shaping future directions, is to reorient the mission of the Church to a practical and immediate cause of liberation. The Church can challenge and transform unjust social or political structures through programs of social empowerment. The Church needs to rethink its practical engagement with the world in terms of social action. This should not be understood simply in terms of relief and occasional interventions but as ongoing project that is integral part of mission.

Conclusion: *Quo Vadis*?

Quo Vadis is a Latin phrase which means "where are you going?" The use of this phrase in the Christian tradition goes back to the first century of Christian era. A story is told in the apocryphal book of *Acts of Peter* (Vercelli Acts XXXV) where the risen Lord meets Peter who was fleeing from persecution in Rome. It is then that Jesus asks Peter, 'where are you going?' The encounter left Peter heartbroken for losing focus and direction. He resolved from hence forth to follow Christ courageously, something he did to the very end of his earthly life and eventually accepting martyrdom.

The Church is likened to a sojourner in this world. Occasionally retreating but for most part advancing. There are occasions the church may have lost focus if not direction and should rightly be asked by her Lord, '*Quo Vadis?*' The onus, however, is on the Church to stop in her tracks, from time to time, and re-examine her mission by insisting on the question, 'where are we going?' Mission calls for a habit of continuous self interrogation and assessment as well as a careful crafting of workable strategies that can take the African church well into the future.

Trends like Pentecostalism or charismatic renewal movements may come and go but the church that gets right its orthodoxy, theological depth and contextual relevance; stands the greatest chance to carry the Christian banner well into the future. The Church that affords a better and alternative model for shaping a new social reality, and the Church that can point to infinite possibilities in God's world stands a high chance of writing home a new story of Christianity's real success in Africa.

Two things, however, must always be held together: correct mission and sound theological education. Pentecostalism in Kenya may have found workable mission strategies, but the numbers may not continue growing unless such strategies are informed and shaped by strong theological education.

CHAPTER FIVE

Towards A Conversational Model

Introduction

As was indicated in our brief analysis of the 'state of African Christianity' in chapter one, the African Christian holds a dual loyalty, to Christ on the one hand and to the traditional religions on the other. To address this, we proposed in chapter two the need for a mission that is God-centered and guided and shaped by clear biblical principles. Chapter three pointed to possibilities of a contextually relevant theology and models of theological education that may adequately address the deep disconnects that characterize African Christianity at all levels. It is also evident as shown in chapter four that the future directions of African Christianity will strongly be shaped by doctrinal and evangelistic themes and emphasis that will directly address issues of contextual concerns such as poverty and diseases. In the present chapter, we suggest, although only in a tentative and exploratory way, a 'conversational model' for African Christianity and Theology that can draw together these various threads.

A Conversational Model

Christianity is necessarily dynamic in that the Gospel usually finds a cultural re-expression in every new context and historical setting. Andrew Walls, observing this dynamic nature of Christianity writes:

> ...The desire to 'indigenize,' to live as a Christian and yet as a member of one's own society, to make the church ... a place to feel

> at home. The desire to do this is tied up with the very nature of the Gospel; it is patterned in the incarnation itself. When God became man, Christ took flesh in a particular family, members of a particular nation, with the tradition and customs associated with that nation. All that was not evil he sanctified.[1]

Andrew Walls in the above quote observes that when the Gospel encounters a new culture, it does not only find a new cultural expression but also becomes the judge to vet all that is evil. We submit that Jesus, the subject of the Gospel becomes the norm against which all other standards are judged. The judgment comes in the form of a critical evaluation of the cultural beliefs and practices, and helpfully takes an exploratory and conversational approach. Such an approach is most fruitful in establishing the root causes of disturbing disconnects that exist between doctrine and ethics, theology and morality, and generally, faith claims and practice. The model of 'learning theology' in dialogue or conversation, with an eye on the text and the other on the context, is what we shall explore as our way of synthesizing the thoughts of the preceding four brief chapters.

As we argued in chapter two, God's mission model is incarnational and that correctly caught, mission is *Missio Dei*. God is a God who takes residence in a particular human culture and reveals himself from within the host culture. The canonical scripture is the primary witness to God's self revelation, and so becomes the key source for all Christian theology, their contextual specificity notwithstanding. The primary witnesses tell their story from the perspectives of a particular historical setting, cultural setting and human experiences or situations in life. When the Gospel is read in a new context, the stories of the primary witnesses stand side by side with the experiences, beliefs, nuances, practices, stories and contextual situations of the hearers. There is an obvious need to bring the text and context into conversation with one another. It may

---

[1] "The Gospel as the Prisoner and Liberator of Culture," *Missionalia* 10:3, 1982, 93 – 105 at 97.

be true that these voices and stories from different milieus and varied fusion of horizons may find a common point of experience, similarity of conditions in life, share the same or similar kind of struggles, fears, anxieties, hopes and expectations, joy and sorrow, love and hate, embrace and exclusion or acceptance and rejection. It is still likely, however, that what in chapter three above we called 'hermeneutical gap' may determine a varied understanding and application of such shared concepts. How best can we bring the two, text and the context into conversation?

The Gospel in Conversation with the Context
Helpful lines of development with regard to how the Gospel may engage culture, or the general context that broadly includes traditional beliefs and all forms of life situations have been explored to a great length and depth by many eminent African theologians. Such models as adaptation, indigenization, inculturation and liberation have been employed in an attempt to answer the question of how best the gospel may find a fruitful reception within the African context and cultural setting.[2] Although all these models are commendable, there is yet a disturbing disconnect between lofty proposals by scholars and the actual application of the proposed models or the appropriation of the same by the grass-root communities of faith. It is in this light that I am proposing what we simply called a 'conversational model' of reading scripture. This means interpreting scriptures with (not for) the Christians who read and understand scriptures in their own ways as informed by their particular cultural setting and situations in life.

If the canonical scripture is the key or primary source of our theology, and if the scripture occupies such a prominent place in the lives of African Christians, it is imperative that the Church must wrestle with the question of biblical interpretation. As noted in chapter three, Western models of interpretation and especially the

---

[2]For an excellent treatment of the subject, see, for example, Stephen B. Bevans *Models of Contextual Theology*, (Maryknoll, NY: Orbis, 2002).

historical critical methods of biblical interpretations have been dominant on the African scene. On the other hand, there are, a variety of 'contextual biblical interpretations' being generated from the readings by the grass-root faith communities. Some approaches, generally common among most of the grass-root communities include, but not exclusively, narratory, literalistic and allegorical methods of interpretations. The historicity of every biblical story is assumed even when allegorical interpretation is applied.

Although these methods do not always do justice to the text, they are, nevertheless, not completely without their benefit. The literalistic method, for example, although simplistic, is helpful when related to problems that the reader (or hearer) experiences in daily life. It helps to correct, a neutral over-spiritualized interpretation that usually ignores the physical needs of the reader. Its strength is particularly in its creative possibilities that can afford conversational engagements between the world of the text and that of the reader. We recommend that the Church needs to read the scriptures, not for, but with the grass-root communities of faith, and tap into the rich hermeneutical shades that arise. An inter-textual approach to the scripture itself could also help draw hermeneutical boundaries that can helpfully guide against erroneous interpretations. The end goal of conversational model is the realization of a credible long-life project of contextual bible reading. The approach affords the meeting of horizons where shared stories will help clarify the criteria for a fruitful living built on the two dimensional law of love of God and that of neighbor. A good example of this in theological education is the African churches' Theological Education by Extension (TEE) model. Despite numerous shortcomings, TEE can afford a good opportunity for conversational model of scriptural interpretation.

The Academy in Conversation with the Church

Another area of fruitful engagement would be an on-going conversation between the academy and the Church. In chapter three, we proposed what we called a 'project model' for theological and spiritual formation as necessary not only for the leaders of the church but also the whole church. The project model basically anticipates a life-long learning process of formation. It involves the formation of, among other things, conversation partners and 'formation paths.' It must be admitted that the traditional settings for the ministerial, theological and spiritual formation, like the seminary or the university, are not exclusive avenues for 'learning and teaching of theology.' The traditional setting is not also always in synch with the cultural and religious circumstances, as well as the contextual realities of the grass-root faith communities.

This is so, mainly because there is often a gap between the academies (the settings of these formations) and the churches for which the academies train church leaders. There is an urgent need for the two to adopt a 'conversational model' of training that is built on partnership. The academy can provide resources and the context for engaging with the traditional sources of theology (scripture, Christian traditions, creeds and philosophies that are a distillation of human wisdom and reason but also witnesses to God's self revelation); and the pastoral setting can provide a conversational partner for theologians and thereby generate theological questions and agenda. Such conversations can in turn inform theological reflection and help develop relevant theological curricula to meet the needs of specific pastoral contexts. It will also help address the awkward situation where academies usually end up busy providing answers to questions no one in particular is asking.

The conversational model should be made formal and structured; and aimed at providing theological formation for the whole church of Christ as opposed to a theological class composed of theologians to avoid theological elitism and clericalism. In this case, both facilitator and the grass-root communities of ones' pastoral context become the conversational partners together with the learners. Formation then becomes interactive, informative as well as interrogative raising questions arising from real life situations and shaping theological reflection in light of the traditional sources of Christian theology (mainly the Scriptures and the Fathers).

The 'conversational model' of formation should be open-ended and not limited to prescribed timeframe. It should ideally be lifelong and cyclic in nature where periodic engagement with the academy and the pastoral community of conversation becomes a continuous process. We offer that a continuous dialogical engagement is fruitful, especially in as far as it bears on the sources of theology, shapes a contextual hermeneutic and aids a deep theological reflection that is thoroughly contextual and at the same time biblical.

An Inter-Church Conversation

In chapter four we delineated how contextual realities are shaping particular doctrinal themes, evangelistic enterprise and emphases. The Churches' responses to contextual needs have seen the rise and phenomenal growth of brands of Christianity such as Pentecostalism and neo-Pentecostalism including charismatic movements in the mainline churches. These brands of Christianity are often characterized by the shallowness of their theology (with leaders often lacking formal theological training); but also doctrinal pitfalls and weak ecclesiastical structures. Yet they have proved to our puzzlement that their brand of Christianity is among the most attractive religious movements of our times. This is an indication that there must be something that they are doing right. We argued that their common emphases on the liberating power of the Gospel as well as their realistic approach to issues that face the faithful on daily basis are their particular strength. This gives Pentecostalism a competitive edge over other churches. It also means that, the churches, across various doctrinal, theological, traditional and historical divides have a lot to learn from each other and can afford excellent opportunities for conversational partnerships.

The traditional (mainline) churches have a wealth of theological resources although it will do better if these churches paid more attention to the question of: 'how theology may be made more relevant for the present African context.' These churches also possess huge doctrinal and liturgical strength that could be offered to the whole universal church of Christ. The doctrinal, theological and liturgical strengths of the mainline churches and their rich historical traditions, on one hand, and the evangelistic, contextual and numerical strength of the Pentecostal churches can be brought into a partnership based on an inter-church conversational approach to mission and evangelism. As explained below, various forms of conversations are already taking place although really inadvertent, informal and unstructured.

The Pentecostal churches are seen to borrow, for example, more and more from the ecclesiastical structure, administrative and constitutional arrangements of the mainline churches, especially at a stage of growth where a given Pentecostal church becomes more established. One particular observation is of their characteristic shift from congregationalism form of governance to a more structured Episcopal form (Kenyan examples is here a case in point). The mainline churches, on the other hand, have largely taken to liturgical innovations where they tend more and more towards Pentecostal spirituality in their worship and discipleship strategies and methods. These churches' effort to contain the charismatic and revivalist movements within their ranks is an indication of an on-going conversation, an internal negotiation with the 'Pentecostalism within,' although for most part only informally and at times even reactionary.

If these conversations are made more deliberate and structured, it will surely promote the theological, doctrinal and liturgical strength of the church in Africa. One other advantage of formalizing such conversation is the potential that the African church can begin to overcome the artificially denominational divides in which the church historically found itself. With deliberate and guided inter-church conversations especially in doctrine, theology and liturgy, there is always great potential to find a way that Christianity can become a truly African religion that is grounded both in context and in the gospel of Christ.

Conclusion

We have proposed 'conversational model' for practical benefits that it can afford. Conversation Model is bound to be reflective and critical. It also affords opportunity of engagement across contexts and interrogates the value of our doctrines and practical demands of such doctrines. It also helps clarify various points of view and cultivates understanding across contexts. It is in this last sense that conversational model can be really fruitful in the shaping and the realization of a model of a social reality, practical Christian communion and a just society.

CHAPTER SIX

Conclusion

Christianity is widely followed in Africa yet African Christianity is generally 'superficial' and suffers from serious disconnects at various levels. Given that the phenomenal numerical growth has failed to translate into maturity of faith and theological strength, there is then the need to seriously revisit the ways the 'churches' have conducted their mission and taught theology.

African Christianity needs a methodological framework that can effectively aid theological reflection, ethical and doctrinal demands of the Christian faith, the interpretation of scriptures, and of how the message of the gospel can correctly be appropriated and applied in the face of varied contextual realities that face the African Christian on daily basis. There is need for systematic reflection on the original sources of Christianity, with the aim to generate a genuine conversation between text and context.

The outcome of such conversational engagement is hoped to lead to the realization of an orthodox and contextually relevant theology and a biblically based mission, which can effectively address the pastoral concerns of the church in fruitful ways that can bring about the abundance of life that the Gospel promises. To aid our explorations in this direction, we have proposed a conversational model of doing theology. The conversational model suggests a reflective engagement at various levels, including conversations between church and academic as well an inter-church dialogue. It is hoped that such engagement will inspire exchange, understanding and models for practical Christian living that integrates doctrine, ethics and such other practical demands of the Gospel.

Sound theological education, and workable mission strategies guided by biblical principles can go a long way in shaping Christianity that can bring about the realization of societal transformation and abundance of life. Pentecostalism seems to be beginning to shape African Christianity in a big way. With its message of liberation and emphases on heaven but also earthly benefits of the Gospel, it carries a great potential to inspire a new social vision that can help in the realization of societal transformation for peace, prosperity, social justice and equity, security and holistic human progress in Africa.

Bibliography

Altizer, Thomas, J. J. 1997. *The Contemporary Jesus:* SCM Press.
Anderson, Allan. 2005. "New African Initiated Pentecostalism and Charismatics in South Africa." *Journal of Religion in Africa*, 35 (1): 68-92.
Anderson, Allan., 2000. *Zion and Pentecost: the Spirituality and Experience of Pentecostal and Zionist/Apostolic Churches of South Africa*, Tshwane: University of South Africa.
Barret, D. B. (ed.) 1982. *World Christian Encyclopedia* OUP, Nairobi.
Bevans, Stephen B., 2002. *Models of Contextual Theology*, Orbis, Maryknoll, NY.
Bloch-Hoell, Nils, 1964. *The Pentecostal Movement: Its Origin, Development and Distinctive Character* London: Allen & Unwin.
Boff, Leonardo, 1978. *Jesus Christ the Liberator*. Maryknoll, New York: Orbis.
Borg, Marcus, 1994. *Jesus in Contemporary Scholarship*. Trinity Press International, Harrisburg.
Bray, Gerald, 1984. *Creeds, Councils and Christ* Leceister, IVP.
Brown, Colin, 1968. *Philosophy and the Christian Faith* Leicester: IVP.
Bujo, Benezet, 1992. *African Theology in its Social Context*, Pauline Press, Nairobi.
Burgess Stanley M., and McGee Gary B. (eds.), 1988. *Dictionary of Pentecostal and Charismatic Movements* Grand Rapids, Michigan: Zondervan Publishing House.

Chopp, Rebecca, 1986. *The Praxis of Suffering: An Interpretation of Liberation and Political Theologies* Maryknoll, New York: Orbis.

Cox, Harvey, 1995. *Fire from Heaven* Reading, Massachusetts: Perseus Books.

Dyrness, William A., 1990. *Learning about Theology from the Third World*, Zondervan.

Fielding, Charles, "Where do ministers come from? Some thoughts on models of theological education" accessed online at: *htt://goliath.acnext.com/com2*; May 2010.

Ford, David F., 2007. *Christian Wisdom: Desiring God and Learning in Love*, CUP Cambridge.

Galgalo and Mombo, "Theological Education and Ecumenical Formation: Some Challenges," *Ecumenical Formation* July/October 2002 vol.98/99, 7-14

Galgalo, J. D. and LeMarquand, G; eds. 2004. *Theological Education in Contemporary Africa*. Zapf Chancery, Eldoret.

Getui, Mary and Theuri, Matthew (eds) 2001. *Quest for Abundant Life in Africa*. Acton Publishers, Nairobi.

Gutierrez, Gustavo, 1993. *La Casas: In Search of the Poor of Jesus Christ* Maryknoll, New York: Orbis.

Healey, Joseph and Sybertz, Donald, 1996. *Towards an African Narrative Theology*. Pauline Publications, Nairobi.

Hennelly, Alfred T. (ed)., 1990. *Liberation Theology: A Documented History* New York: Orbis.

Hinga, Teresa M., 1992. "Jesus Christ and the Liberation of Women in Africa," in Mercy Amba Oduyoye and Musimbi R A Kanyoro (eds.) *The Will to Arise* Maryknoll, New York: Orbis,

Hollenweger, Walter J., 1972. *The Pentecostals* London: SCM Press.

Hollenweger, Walter J., 1990. "The Theological challenge of Indigenous Churches," in Walls, A.F. and Shenk, W.R. (eds.) *Exploring New Religious Movements* Elkhart: Mission Focus Publications, 163-67

Inbody, Tyron, I., 2002. *The Many Faces of Christology*. Abingdon Press, Nashville.

Jenkins, Philip, 2002. *The Next Christendom: The Coming of Global Christianity* Oxford: OUP.
Katongole, Emmanuel, 2010. *The Sacrifice of Africa: A Political Theology for Africa*. Grand Rapids: Eerdmans.
Kevin and Dorothy Ranaghan, 1969. *Catholic Pentecostals* NY: Paulist Press.
Küster, Volker, 1999. *The Many Faces of Jesus Christ* Maryknoll, New York: Orbis.
Lai, Wilfred "The Power of the Tongue," A sermon preached at his Mombasa "*Jesus Celebration Centre*," and broadcast on KTN on Sunday 9, February 2003 at 8.00 am.
Maimela, Simon, 1986. "Current Themes and Emphases in Black Theology," in Itumeleng Mosala and Buti Tlhagale (eds.), *The Unquestionable Right to be Free* Maryknoll, NY: Orbis.
Martney, Emmanuel, 1993. *African Theology: Inculturation and Liberation* Maryknoll, New York: Orbis.
McGee, et al (eds.) *Dictionary of Charismatic Movements* Grand Rapids, Michigan: Zondervan .
McGee, Gary, 1993. "Pentecostal and Charismatic Missions," in Philips, James and Coote, Robert (eds.), *Toward the 21st Century in Christian Mission*, Michigan: Eerdmans, 41-53.
Michael C. Griffiths, "Theological Education Need Not be Irrelevant," *Vox Evangelica* 20 (1990): 7- 20.
Mugambi, J. N. K., 1995. *From Liberation to Reconstruction: African Christian Theology after the Cold War* Nairobi: E.A. Publishing House.
Mugambi, J. N. K., 2002. "From Liberation to Reconstruction," in Emmanuel Katangole (ed.) *African Theology Today* Scranton: The University of Scranton Press.
Oden, Thomas C., 2008. *How Africa Shaped the Christian Mind: Rediscovering the African Seedbed of Western Christianity*. Downers Grove, Ill.: InterVarsity.
Ombuor, Joe and Ikonya, Philo, 1999. "Clerics' Lavish Living," in "Your Weekender Magazine," *Daily Nation*, Friday, March 19, Nairobi.

Otto F. A. Meinardus, 2002. *Two Thousand Years of Coptic Christianity*, American University, Cairo Press.

Pala, Oyunga, 2003. "Make a Million by Hook or Crook," *Saturday Nation*, February 15-21, Nairobi

Parratt, John, 1995. *Reinventing Christianity*. Grand Rapids: Eerdmans.

Paul H Gundani et al; "The State of Theological Education in Southern Africa: Issues and Concerns," *Ecumenical Formation* July/October 2002 vol.98/99, 67-75.

Pelikan, Jaroslav, 1998. *Jesus through the Centuries: His Place in the History of Culture*. Yale University Press.

Peter, C.B., "The Churches Response to Poverty: A Jungian Appraisal of the "Prosperity Gospel" Phenomenon," in *Ogbomoso Journal of Theology* Vol. XIV, 2009:137-147.

Peter, C. B., 1994. "African Hyphenated Christians – an Alternate Model of Theologizing in Africa," in *Nordic Journal of African Studies* 3(1), 100 – 113.

Petersen, Douglas., 1996. *Not by Might Nor by Power: A Pentecostal Theology of Social Concern in Latin America*, Regnum, Oxford.

Philips, James and Coote, Robert (eds.), 1993. *Toward the 21st Century in Christian Mission*, Michigan: Eerdmans.

Schreiter, Robert J., 1985. *Constructing Local Theologies*, Orbis.

Shorter, Alyward and Njiru, 2001. Joseph *New Religious Movements in Africa* Nairobi: Pauline Publications.

Shorter, Aylward, 1996. *Christianity and the African Imagination: After the African Synod Resources for Inculturation* Pauline Press, Nairobi.

Sievernich, Michael, 2011. *Christian Mission*, Mainz: Institute of European History.

Sobrino, Jon, 1978. *Christology at the Crossroads* Maryknoll, New York: Orbis.

Spittler, Russell P., 1985. "Children of the Twentieth Century," in Robin Keeley (org. ed.), *The Quiet Revolution* Oxford: Lion Publishers.

Walls, Andrew, 1982. "The Gospel as the Prisoner and Liberator of Culture," *Missionalia* 10:3, 93 – 105, 97.

Wanjiru, Margaret "The Purpose of Jesus' Anointing," a sermon broadcast on KBC Television Saturday, 8 February, 2003 at 8.30 pm.

Ward, J.W., 1994. "Pentecostalist Theology," in *New Dictionary of Theology* Leicester: IVP, 502-505

Wessels, Anton, 1990. *Images of Jesus: How Jesus is Perceived and Portrayed in Non-European Cultures*. London: SCM.

Wilson, D. J. 1988. "Pentecostal Perspectives on Eschatology," in Stanley M Burgess et al (eds.) *Dictionary of Pentecostal and Charismatic Movements* Michigan: Zondervan Publishing, 345-49.

Wink, Walter; 1983. *The Bible in Human Transformation*. Fortress Press.

Yung, Hwa, 1997. *Mangos or Bananas? The Quest for an Authentic Asian Christian Theology*. Regnum Books, New Delhi.

African Christianity: The Stranger Within

Index of Personal Names

Altizer, Thomas J. J., 75
Anton Wessels, 20

Barth, Karl 69
Bevans, Stephen B., 101
Boulaga, Fabien Eboussi, 17
Bray, Gerald Creeds, 39, 56
Burgess, Stanley M., 81

Feuerbach, Ludwig 44

Galgalo, J. D., 54, 60, 61
Griffiths, Michael C., 60, 62
Gutierrez, Gustavo, 73, 74

Harvey, Cox, 83, 94
Hennelley, Alfred T., 75
Hinga, Teresa M., 78, 79
Hollenweger, Walter J., 92, 93

Jenkins, Philip, 80, 85, 86, 87, 88, 90

Kanyoro, Musimbi R. A., 78, 79
Karanja, J. K., 21, 22

Keeley, Robin, 81

LeMarquand, G., 54, 61

Martey, Emmanuel, 66,
Mbiti, J. S., 70
McGee, Gay B., 81
Meinardus, Otto F. A., 81
Mombo, 60

Njiru, 85, 88, 89

Oduyoye, Mercy Amba, 78, 79

Parratt, John 55
Peter, C.B. 12, 49, 50, 51, 52, 53

Schreiter, Robert, 71
Shorter, 85, 88, 89
Sievernich, Michael, 39
Spittler, Russell P., 81

Wilson, D. J. 92
Wright, Christopher, J. H. 32, 33

Auditing Priniples: A Stuents' Handbook by **Musa O. Nyakora (2007)**
The Concept of Botho *and HIV/AIDS in Botswana* edited **by Joseph B. R. Gaie and Sana K. MMolai (2007)**
Captive of Fate: A Novel by **Ketty Arucy (2007)**
A Guide to Ethics by **Joseph Njino (2008)**
Pastoral Theology: Rediscovering African Models and Methods by **Ndung'u John Brown Ikenye (2009)**
The Royal Son: Balancing Barthian and African Christologies by **Zablon Bundi Mutongu (2009)**
AIDS, Sexuality, and Gender: Experiencing of Women in Kenyan Universities by **Nyokabi Kamau (2009)**
Modern Facilitation and Training Methodology: A Guide to Best Practice in Africa by **Frederick Chelule (2009)**
How to Write a Winning Thesis by **Simon Kang'ethe et al (2009)**
Absolute Power and Other Stories by **Ambrose Rotich Keitany (2009)**
Y'sdom in Africa: A Personal Journey by **Stanley Kinyeki (2010)**
Abortion and Morality Debate in Africa: A Philosophical Enquiry by **George Kegode (2010)**
The Holy Spirit as Liberator: A Study of Luke 4: 14-30 by **Joseph Koech (2010)**
Biblical Studies, Theology, Religion and Philosophy: An Introduction for African Universities, **Gen. Ed. James N. Amanze (2010)**
Modeling for Servant-Leaders in Africa: Lessons from St. Paul by **Ndung'u John Brown** Ikenye (2010)
HIV & AIDS, Communication and Secondary Education in Kenya by **Ndeti Ndati (2011)**
Disability, Society and Theology: Voices from Africa by **Samuel Kabue et al (2011)**
If You Have No Voice Just Sing!: Narratives of Women's Lives and Theological Education at St. Paul's University by **Esther Mombo and Heleen Joziasse (2011)**
Mutira Mission: An African Church Comes of Age in Kirinyaga, Kenya (1912-2012) by **Julius Gathogo (2011)**
The Bible and African Culture: Mapping Transactional Inroads by **Humphrey Waweru, (2011)**
Karl Jaspers' Philosophy of Existence: Insights for Out Time by **Cletus N. Chukwu (2011)**
Diet of Worms: Quality of Catering in Kenyan Prisons by **Jacqueline Cheptekkeny Korir (2011)**
Our Father! An Indian Christian Prays the Lord's Prayer by **C. B. Peter (2011)**